ROBERT ERN

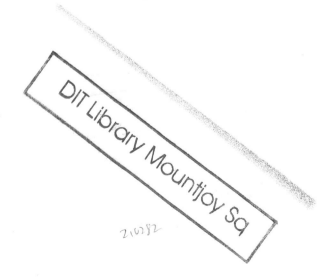

ROBERT A. M. STERN

Buildings and Projects
1993–1998

Edited by Peter Morris Dixon

THE MONACELLI PRESS

First published in the United States of America
in 1998 by
The Monacelli Press, Inc.
10 East 92nd Street
New York, New York 10128.

Library of Congress
Cataloging-in-Publication Data
Stern, Robert A. M.
Robert A. M. Stern : buildings and projects,
1993–1998.
p. cm.
ISBN 1-58093-017-4
1. Stern, Robert A. M. 2. Architecture,
Modern—20th century—United States—
Themes, motives. 3. Interior architecture—
United States. I. Title.
NA737.S64A4   1998
720'.92—dc21   98-29443

Front cover: Residence in Starwood, Aspen,
Colorado, 1991–1996. Photograph: Peter
Aaron/Esto.

Back Cover: Feature Animation Building,
The Walt Disney Company, Burbank,
California, 1991–1994. Photograph: Peter
Aaron/Esto © The Walt Disney Company,
used by permission.

Printed and bound in Italy

Designed by Abigail Sturges

Contents

Introduction

Robert A. M. Stern

It is not being the first to see something new that indicates a genuinely original mind, but seeing the old, the familiar, the commonplace as if it were new.

—Friedrich Nietzsche,
  Human, All Too Human: A Book for Free Spirits

Contemporary practice and theory remind me of the pop song "Fifty Ways to Leave Your Lover": they do anything but confront a situation head-on. When architects meet to discuss their art they pose issue after issue in a restless search to avoid addressing the simple but profound circumstances of architecture. These "issues" include literary theory and social science, cyberspace and many more. But what of architecture itself? For me, architecture is enough—difficult but full of possibilities. For me, architecture is an expression of the real world—the built world in the service of individuals and institutions. It is the art of construction, not deconstruction; of representation, not communication. It is the solidity of the here-and-now. Put another way, architecture is the stage on which humanity plays out its ever-changing drama. It is the stage, not the drama; the setting, not the performer. It is not inhabited sculpture, or drawings, or performance, to name but a few of the things it is often confused with, especially by architects seeking to "push" their art. Architecture need only be itself to interest me; indeed it need only be true to itself to be true. To ask it to be other things, to blend it with writing or painting or dance or whatever, is to diminish its power and shirk its responsibilities. Architecture is interesting and valuable enough for what it is and for the process of its making, from the first conversations with the client through the thinking and research that takes place in the studio to the actual realization on a site. These are what architecture is, and the glory of what architecture is. As we build each building we add to architecture—or try to. As we shape each design, modifying what went before, adding what meets a particular need—one that was discovered, not willed—architecture is enriched and our own contribution is made.

The twentieth century's battle of the styles, between the modernists and the traditionalists, seems as far from conclusion as it ever was—simply because it cannot be won by either side. To be modern, which we are compelled to be by the inescapable facts of historical circumstance, we must incorporate the new; but to be modern we must also cultivate tradition, lest we drown in the placeless materialism of an architecture that without a past would all too easily surrender our humanistic values to those of a continually evolving materialism and now, with electronic technologies, those of an even more provoking and troubling dematerialism. Convinced that the continued stylistic battle is inherently futile and foolish, I prefer to concentrate on other aspects of the building art. I prefer to establish or reinforce a sense of place by creating spatial order amid the chaos of a fast-changing world (too many of my colleagues seem to favor a studied disorder). I work to bring not only order but also intimacy of feeling to even the largest projects. For this reason the design of houses and small institutional buildings continues to be not only a pleasurable part of my work but a self-imposed discipline, a "control" (as in a laboratory experiment) by which I measure in human terms the success of the commissions for large buildings that have increasingly come to our practice in recent years.

In earlier volumes on our firm I outlined the underlying principles behind the work, which still seem to hold: the conviction that the inherent iconoclasm of modernism combined with its pseudoscientific approach (which once obsessed over the shapes of machines and which today seeks to substitute communications technology for solid form) compromises, perhaps even abrogates, architecture's grand purpose—the physical definition of space and place. Architecture is not a branch of engineering or communications science. It is a social art, a public art. Moreover, it is fixed in place.

Notwithstanding my quarrel with any technologically determined or formally reductive approach to architecture, I am no Luddite. I admire and continue to learn from what our great engineers accomplish, and I remain impressed with the high-wire modernism of the great formalists of our century's middle years: Le Corbusier and Mies van der Rohe. But as I write this I am moved to observe that the high-wire modernism of the 1920s and 1930s that shaped my education in the late 1950s and early 1960s was very different from the modernism of today: traditional architecture was inextricably part of the glory years of the modern movement, as Le Corbusier made clear in his polemical writings and Reyner Banham reiterated in his book *Theory and Design in the First Machine Age.* Modernism was a stylistic rebellion against what it regarded as the outmoded classicism of the Ecole des Beaux-Arts. Yet, as Banham demonstrated, the formulators of the new modernist style, particularly Le Corbusier, wanted to remake the academic tradition in their own image, not to overthrow the tradition itself. They valued its underlying discipline, its rigor. They regarded the past as a standard of measure for the present, and they often usurped its artifacts for their own purposes. In short, they wanted to reform architectural expression, not to abandon architecture as a whole. Today's modernism, at least as one sees it in the studios of the leading architectural schools, seems in no way interested in the underlying framework of architecture. Indeed, it has virtually abandoned the hitherto key— indeed basic—issues: composition, humanistic proportion, and, above all, the deep concern with functional expression represented in solid form that must be at the heart of responsible building. For too many young architects, architecture seems best only when it is at the margin— so close to the edge, in fact, that it runs the risk of falling over the precipice and becoming something else. What that "else" might be is not clear, but I have a sinking feeling that, once discovered, it will not be architecture.

I continue to believe in what I have in an earlier volume on our practice labeled modern traditionalism: neither a return to the past nor a pseudo-innocent amnesia but a constantly renewing architecture with its feet firmly planted in the continuum of the building art. In every way our work is modern: in its programs, in its scale, materials, and structure—and, most importantly, in its positive embrace of the complex and largely contradictory realities of postindustrial society. Our forms may be old or new, but our attitude is entirely modern, because the so-called global village has brought with it a pressing need to protect the specifics of place and local culture in the face of the onslaught of mass communications and mass tourism, to mention but two aspects of late-twentieth-century society that most directly threaten to homogenize human experience.

Architecture is diminished by buildings that express a fixed, predetermined idea. Born of practical consideration of function and tectonics, architecture molds shapes, sounds, and light to invoke specific reactions of pleasure. In different places and countries where work takes me and my partners, I welcome the opportunity to discover the threads of traditional cultures, all too often lost or broken. I welcome the global outreach of today's practice, which further enables me to fulfill my commitment to an architecture that is neither about personal style nor universal and therefore inherently placeless, but one that tries to be engaged with, rooted in, place. Despite the effort to have our buildings "fit in," I do not think they do so in an anonymous way. Nor do I believe that our buildings are the expression of some sort of present-day "born-again" vernacular. They are sincere contributions to the local scene and, as such, are necessarily self-conscious, deliberate comments and, where necessary, critiques. On occasion our buildings "fit in" so well that they nearly disappear into the scene. If they sometimes require a second glance to establish their newness in an established context, so be it. "Second-glance" architecture, with all the pleasures of discovery that go with such subtlety, seems far better than the empty gesticulations and polemical posturings of so much self-declamatory contemporary work. Architecture is the setting for life; it is not life itself. Sometimes there is such a thing as too much architecture. More frequently, there is such a thing as too much innovation. Invention, however, that is, the reimagining of basic themes, is always in short supply. My search continues for an architecture that succeeds by virtue of its ability to be new yet somehow old; to be present and absent but not glaringly obtrusive; to be the setting and not the performance in the theater of our lives.

This is the fourth in a series of chronological compilations systematically documenting my work and that of the partners and close associates without whom it could not be realized. The projects in this volume represent a testing of our abilities to build upon the foundations of past work while increasing the scale and the scope of buildings undertaken. A record of projects brought to fruition, never constructed, and currently underway, this book is also a reaffirmation of the ideals and standards

I set for myself—for an architecture that looks to the past in order to shape the present.

The work in this book differs from that in its predecessors not in approach but in sheer volume. The maturity of our practice and the current prosperity have brought many opportunities to build. Yet I have endeavored to hold onto the core vision that has informed the work in the past. The challenge to keep fresh and focused is paramount. To do so, it is essential to be surrounded by a solid structure of collaborative effort. I am privileged to be the leader of a partnership of talented and dedicated architects who share my vision and build upon it: Robert S. Buford, managing partner, who sees to it that the business part of architecture runs smoothly so that the art part can have its proper chance; Roger Seifter, Paul Whalen, and Graham Wyatt, partners, and Arthur Chabon, Randy Correll, Alexander Lamis, Armand LeGardeur, Grant Marani, and Barry Rice, associate partners, who work side by side with me to design the buildings and plan the towns. We carry forward this work with the help of associates of the firm, younger architects, landscape architects, and designers whose individual talents add so much more: Adam Anuszkiewicz, Augusta Barone, John Berson, Gary Brewer, Charlotte Frieze, John Gilmer, Preston Gumberich, Michael Jones, Daniel Lobitz, Raúl Morillas, Geoffrey Mouen, Patricia Burns Ross, Diane Scott, and Ann Stokes.

Buildings and Projects
1993–1998

Architects' Office

New York, New York
1994–1995

12 In 1995 we relocated to larger quarters overlooking the Hudson River and the midtown skyline. As in our previous home, which was also in a converted industrial loft building, the design is a metaphor for the philosophical structure of our practice: a fixed classical core encircled by the open spaces of modernity. The library, a tool and talisman, is at the heart of the workspace, as it is of the firm's design approach—and architects and visitors alike must pass through it again and again as they move about the office. In order to heighten the contrast between the building structure and the architects' interventions, virtually all the new construction was kept independent of the window walls and the ceiling, which were left as found. This also saved money, a fact not lost on many clients; others, unnerved a bit by the bareness, are reassured by the Doric columns and elaborate moldings of the entrance lobby and by the superscaled Doric "table" lamps.

1. Plan
2. View from library toward south

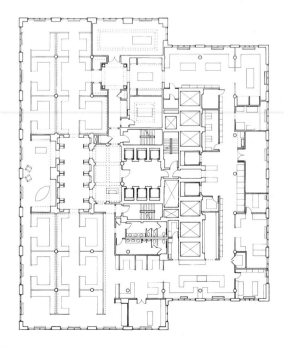

0   10   20   40 ft

1

2

3

4

3. North drafting area
4. Reception area
5. Robert A. M. Stern's office

Center for Jewish Life, Princeton University

Princeton, New Jersey
1986–1993

16   At the request of the university, which believed it could save money, the Center for Jewish Life was initially designed as two wings added to an existing eighty-year-old Tudorbethan house that had once served as an eating club. When contractors came on board, they confirmed what we had claimed all along: an entirely new building would be cheaper. But when it was agreed to tear the house down, so much had been invested in the original concept that the center's redesign carried forward the original parti, with a central mass housing office, library, and lounge spaces; a dining room in one wing; and a sanctuary, the center's principal religious space, in the other. The sanctuary faces Washington Road, the street traditionally marking the separation between Princeton's academic campus and its surrounding neighborhoods.

1. Site plan
2. South facade
3. Previous house on site
4. Entry

2

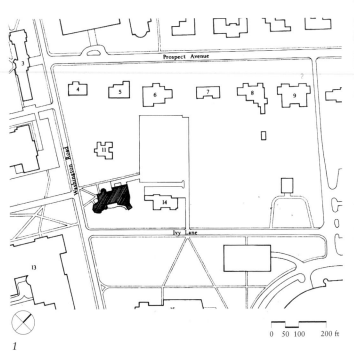

1

0 50 100   200 ft

3

5. Main sanctuary
6. Main stairs
7. Second-floor plan
8. First-floor plan
9. Ground-floor plan
10. Lounge
11. Dining hall
12 (overleaf). South facade

18

5

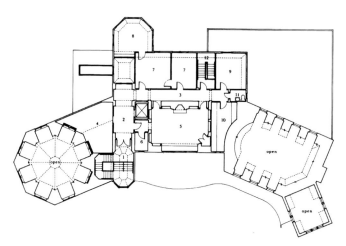

7

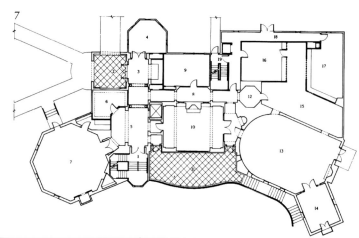

8

6

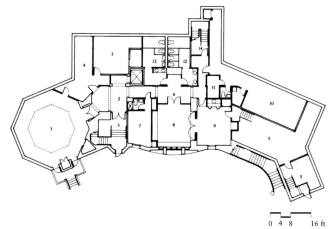

9

0 4 8 16 ft

10

11

Spruce Lodge

Colorado
1987–1991

22   Set atop a knoll along a creek in a valley of the Rocky Mountains, this log and shingle house combines two characteristic American house types—the Adirondack camp and the Rocky Mountain ranch house—to create a picturesque massing of projecting bays and dormers that complements the rugged surroundings and frames spectacular views. The free yet carefully articulated plan opens to the landscape through a combination of screened, covered, and open porches and balconies off the principal rooms, which extend along the southwest facade. Entry is through a porte-cochere into a large vestibule that leads to the double-height living room. Framed with heavy timber trusses, dominated by a Colorado sandstone fireplace, and opening to the view through glass doors and tall windows, this room serves as a grand gathering space at the heart of the house. The second floor is separated by the living room into two wings, one for children and guests and one for the master suite.

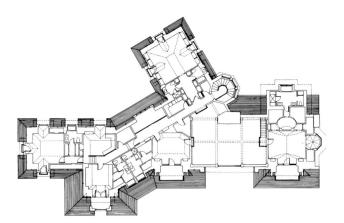

1

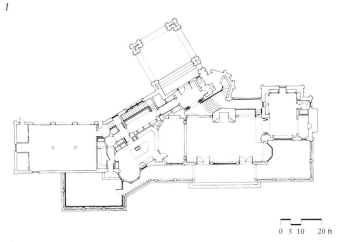

0 5 10   20 ft

2

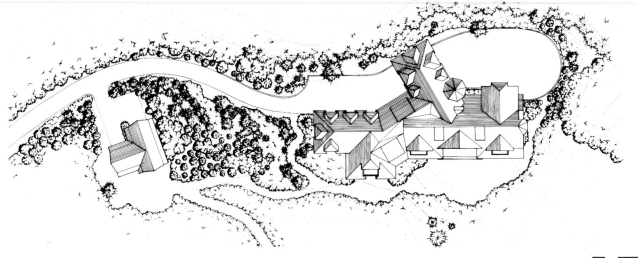

3

0 10 20   40 ft

24

5

6

7

9

9. *View of dining room from main stairway*
10. *Living room*
11. *View of living room with stairway to master bedroom at rear*

10

12. *Dining room*
13. *Guest bedroom*
14. *Bunk room*
15. *View of main stairway from dining room*

28

12

13

14

Norman Rockwell Museum at Stockbridge

Stockbridge, Massachusetts
1987–1993

30 Founded in 1969, the Rockwell Museum was first housed in the Greek Revival–style "corner house" on Stockbridge's Main Street, the preservation of which the artist had championed. By the late 1980s, the museum had grown into a major tourist destination, making it clear that a "proper" building was necessary. Lack of an appropriate site in the village led to the selection of a large property with no particular Rockwell associations a mile or so out of town. To further complicate matters, the site was home to the historic Butler house (1859), which had its own interesting history. As a result, a key aspect of our job was symbolically to connect the new museum with the historic context of Main Street while at the same time being respectful of its equally historic but totally unrelated immediate surroundings.

To enhance the experience of Rockwell's art without compromising the character of the Butler house, the museum is sited away from that structure, views of which are concealed from the arriving visitor, who passes across a surrogate village green—the grassy enclosure of a former cutting garden—to find the museum's cupola-crowned entrance porch. Inside, the museum is organized to provide a clear path of circulation through geometrically resolved gallery spaces. The main galleries, intended for permanent installations, are bathed in natural light. At the building's heart, the top-lit octagonal gallery is dedicated to Rockwell's paintings of the Four Freedoms.

1

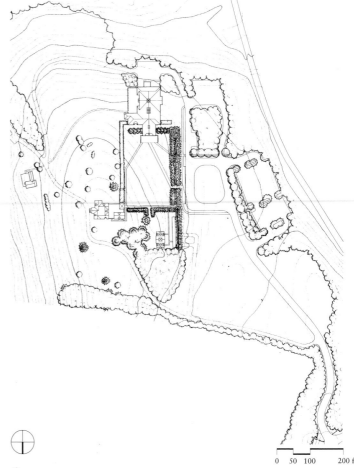

0   50   100   200 ft

2

4

32

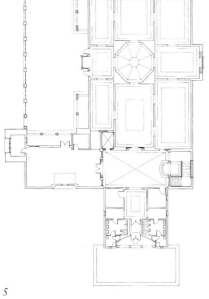

5

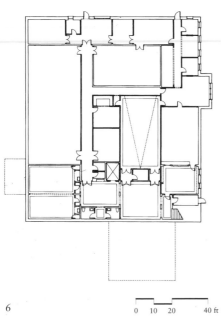

6

0 10 20   40 ft

MY
ADVENTURES
AS AN
ILLUSTRATOR

Residence in River Oaks

Houston, Texas
1988–1992

34   The primary views from this house are northerly, toward the Buffalo Bayou, but the design introduces direct southern light to the principal rooms, which are buffered from the driveway by landscaped, hedge-bounded courtyards. Formal gardens extend the geometry of the house into the grounds in a progression of outdoor rooms starting from the knot garden and leading to the rotunda along the bayou's edge and then to the tennis court and its viewing pavilions.

Climate and local tradition play a strong part in the design: light ochre stucco walls and red-tile roofs work equally well in Houston's intense sun or gray rainy season, and respect the Mediterranean influences seen in some of the area's most interesting architecture. A massing of semidiscrete pavilions and local symmetries, and an ornamental vocabulary of Tuscan details governed by Doric proportions combine to lend scale to the house and also reduce its apparent size.

1. *View of entrance facade from southeast*
2. *First-floor plan*
3. *View of garden facade from northwest*
4. *View from garden toward northeast*

1

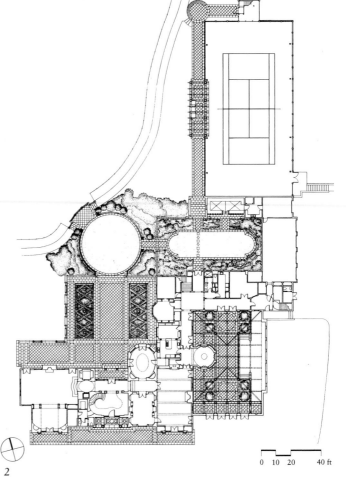

2

0 10 20   40 ft

3

4

7

8

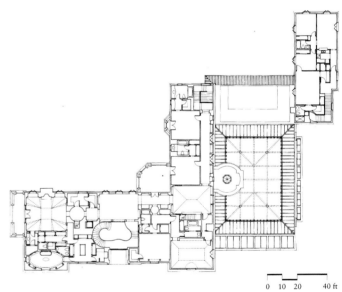

0   10   20   40 ft

9

5

6

5. Stair hall
6. Living-room alcove
7. North elevation
8. South elevation
9. Second-floor plan
10. Gallery

11. *Detail at pool edge*
12. *Cross section through pool entrance*
13. *Pool*

38

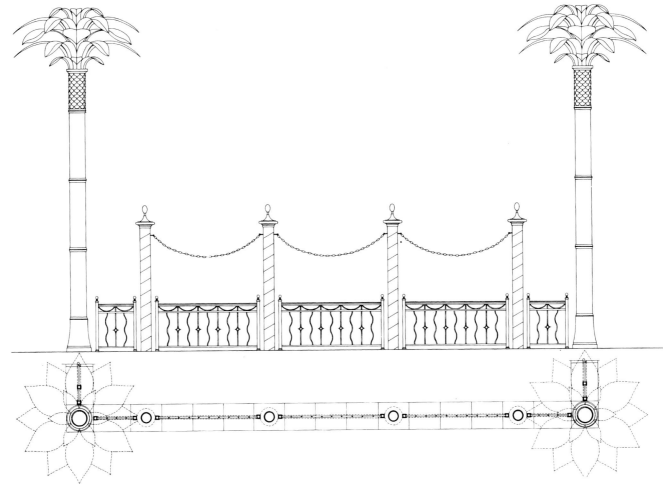

11

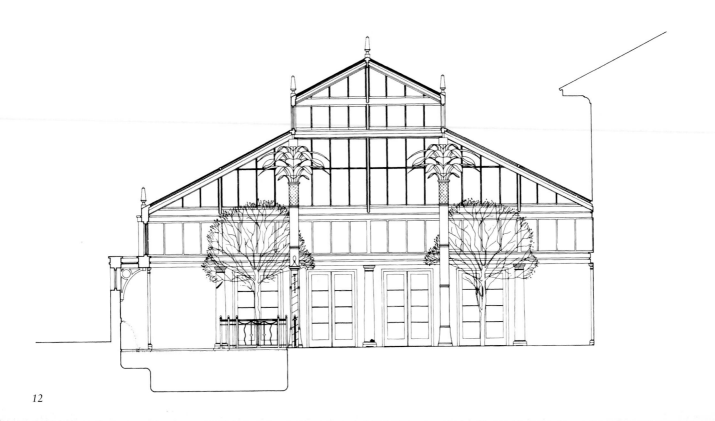

12

Columbus Regional Hospital

Columbus, Indiana
1988–1995

40 At the time we began our work on this project, it could safely be said that most hospitals in America were designed for the efficient delivery of technologically advanced health care but with comparatively little concern for the psychology of the patient and even less for that of close family and other visitors. Moreover, most hospitals had not developed architectural means to present outpatient services to patients, so that, though the actual medical procedure may have been effective, the experience of registering and waiting for treatment was frequently dehumanizing.

Founded in 1917, the Columbus Regional Hospital had grown in a piecemeal fashion to include four hundred thousand haphazardly planned square feet. The hospital made poor use of additional land acquired over the years so that by the mid-1980s it was squeezed into one corner of a thirty-eight-acre site bisected by Haw Creek. At best, the existing complex, which serves a town of thirty thousand and the surrounding region, could be described as a random collection of buildings of various degrees of functional obsolescence. Regrettably, the only architecturally notable building in the complex, the original Italianate structure,

2

1. Site plan showing development history
2. View from west across Haw Creek
3. Ground-floor plan
4. View toward restaurant and outdoor dining terrace

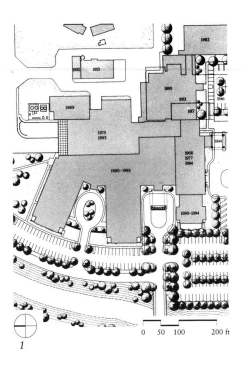

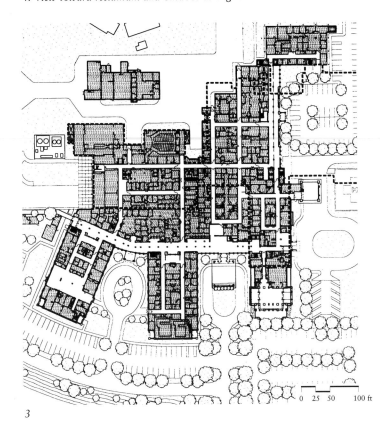

0   50   100   200 ft
1

0   25   50   100 ft
3

5

was not only trapped at the center of an architectural morass but was also hopelessly outmoded.

As redesigned and expanded, the hospital enjoys its parklike site, which is united by a tree-lined entry drive that spans Haw Creek on a new bridge. A pair of thirty-thousand-square-foot medical office buildings, one of which is built, will flank the drive, serving as a symbolic gatehouse. Two-story pavilions and intervening outdoor courtyards are connected by a continuous double-height gallery, so that the overall scale of the facility is broken down to distinctly identifiable but clearly linked elements. Taking cues from hotel design, the extensively glazed, double-height concourse, containing registration and admitting desks, a gift shop, and waiting areas for the hospital's various public departments, acts as the link between the main lobby, emergency suite, and new 180-seat restaurant, which is deliberately placed next to the front to provide a welcoming beacon of light and activity. The low hips of the roofs, containing the mechanical equipment, combined with the warm golden brick trimmed in cast stone, reflect familiar midwestern practice, whether the work of Frank Lloyd Wright, Eliel Saarinen's Kingswood School, or the historic, Italianate Irwin house in the center of town.

5. *Two-story gallery with waiting room beyond*
6. *Admitting-interview cubicle*
7. *Restaurant*
8. *Chapel*

7

8

9. *Main lobby stair*
10. *View of main lobby*
    from second-floor corridor

9

Town Square—Wheaton

Wheaton, Illinois
1988–1992

1. Detail of cornice and sign band
2. Site plan
3. View from northwest
4 (overleaf). View from south
5 (overleaf). Office building from west

46 An "anchorless" suburban retail center, Town Square—Wheaton seeks to lift what is in essence a 160,000-square-foot shopping center to a level of civicism not characteristic of the type. Set amid the placeless sprawl of an affluent western suburb of Chicago, it creates an outdoor room punctuated by freestanding pavilions where food can be served and events staged. Golden-hued brick walls support a painted-wood entablature, cornice, and terra-cotta-colored tile roof, all intending to evoke the early Prairie style work of Frank Lloyd Wright.

1

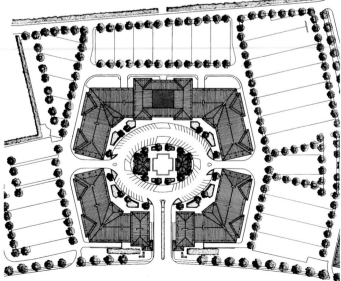

0   50 100   200 ft

2

4, 5

Roger Tory Peterson Institute

Jamestown, New York
1989–1993

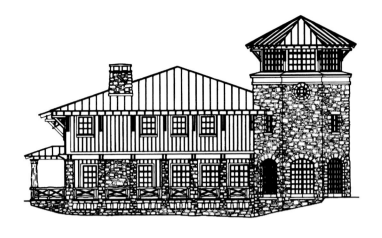

1

50 Built to serve visiting scholars, educators, and small public groups, the Peterson Institute is a center for the study of natural history. The institute is intended to be realized in three stages; the first stage, consisting of a public gallery for the exhibition of wildlife art, an archive for the preservation of wildlife art and rare books on the natural sciences, a library, meeting and conference rooms, and offices, has been completed. Set on an open site at the edge of town, the dynamic composition, comprising geometrically disciplined elements, is articulated with wood and stone to express clearly the institute's environmental mission.

1. *East elevation*
2. *First-floor plan*
3. *Site plan*
4. *North entry facade*
5. *View from entry porch to walled court*
6. *Courtyard pergola*

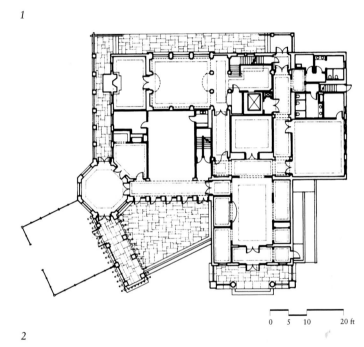

0 5 10   20 ft

2

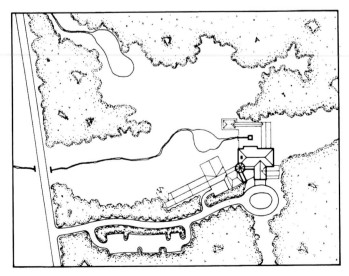

3

0 50 100   200 ft

4

5

6

7. *Upper gallery of main reading room*
8. *Breckenridge Room*
9. *Library stair*
10. *Tower reading room*
11. *Lobby facing south*
12 *(overleaf). Principal (north) facade*

52

7

8

9

10

Anglebrook Golf Club

Somers, New York
1989–1998

56 Some architectural projects, like plutonium, have a half-life. In 1989, as the economy peaked, we designed a thirty-eight-thousand-square-foot clubhouse principally intended for Japanese businesspeople living in the New York area. The shifting economy of the early 1990s, combined with a slow permitting process for the golf course itself, led to a redesign of the project, now somewhat smaller, and its subsequent construction. In distinct contrast to most Japanese clubs, which are quite institutional in scale and character, Anglebrook takes its cue from classic golf clubhouses of Westchester and nearby counties, which typically take the form of large, casually massed country houses.

1. *Main dining room*
2. *Men's locker room*
3. *Site plan*
4. *Main-floor plan*
5. *View of entrance and locker wing from north*
6. *View of dining room and starting terrace from south*

1

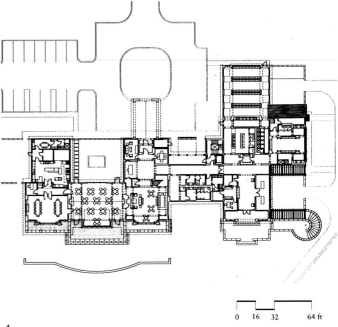

2

0 40 80 160 ft

3

0 16 32 64 ft

4

5

6

House at Apaquogue

East Hampton, New York
1989–1993

58 To fit into its context, this house looks to the local vernacular and the nearby work of Stanford White, who understood better than most how to adapt that vernacular to the requirements of a fairly large program and the delicate scale of the flat landscape of eastern Long Island. Large and small elements are vividly contrasted: rough, thickly cut cedar shakes and bold classical moldings enliven the simple forms of the house; giant pilasters bracket the central entry facade and bear a deep-bracketed eave; slender paired colonettes support the entry porch. Inside, the large rooms open onto one another, exemplifying the kind of country-house planning perfected at the beginning of this century.

1. Site plan
2. South facade
3. West facade

2, 3

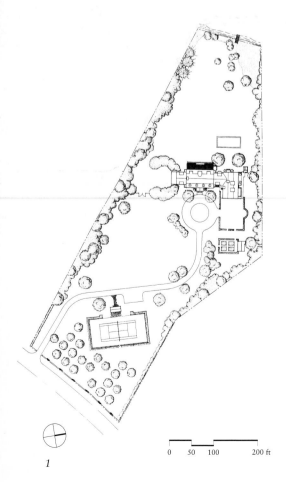

0   50   100   200 ft

1

4

4. *Entrance hall looking toward library*
5. *View from living room into dining room*
6. *First-floor plan*
7. *Living room*
8. *Second-floor plan*

60

5

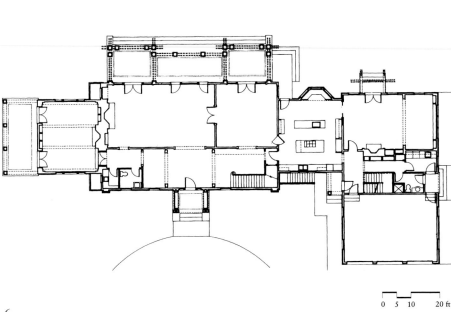

6

0 5 10   20 ft

7

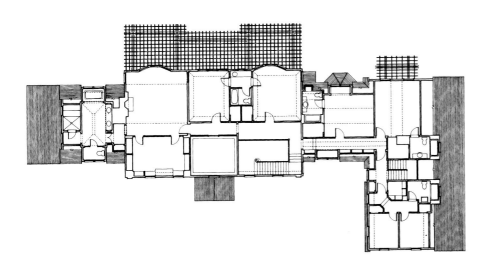

8

62

9. Family room
10. Master bedroom
11. Entrance hall

9

10

Kiawah Beach Club

Kiawah Island, South Carolina
1989–1994

1. Site plan
2. Aerial view of first scheme
3. Principal (north) facade
4. Beach (south) facade

64 The first version of this project—larger and not built—took its design cues from Low Country precedents such as Mulberry, where Georgian classicism mixed with that of the Caribbean. The second version, smaller and more house-like, which has been realized, locks into the Shingle style tradition to suggest the seaside bathing pavilions of the 1890s.

Deep-set covered porches wrap around a double-height dining room. A lower locker wing defines a three-sided court-yard containing the swimming pool. At the outermost corner of this outdoor room, an octagonal "summerhouse" marks the transition between the club grounds and the public beach.

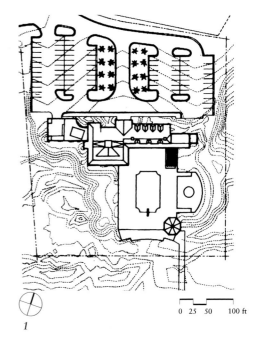

1

0 25 50 100 ft

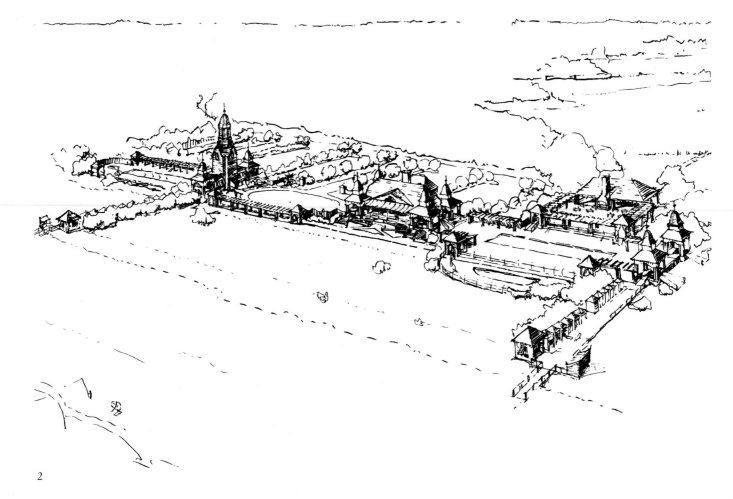

2

3

4

5. *Bay window in lounge*
6. *Beach walkway from summerhouse*
7. *Floor plan*
8. *Dining room*
9 *(overleaf). Evening view looking south
   through dining porch*

5

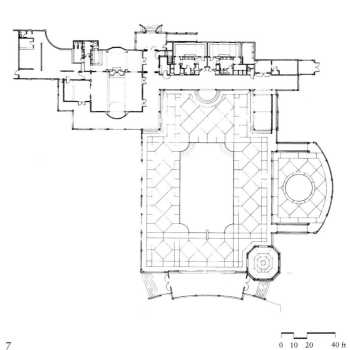

7

0 10 20   40 ft

6

Greenbrier at West Village Golf Resort

Fukushima Prefecture, Japan
1990–1995

70   Virtually all new large-scale construction in Japan eschews any direct connection with the country's building traditions. Our status as outsiders has given us some liberty to ask questions about Japan's architectural past and its relationship to traditions in the West. In the case of the West Village project a dialogue across cultures was particularly appropriate, given our Japanese client's intention to establish an international resort destination reflecting local custom while appealing to both Japanese and international guests. To be cosmopolitan and local at the same time, we mixed Western classical planning with a building form that at first glance may also seem Western but is, in fact, inspired by traditional Japan—not the familiar low-scale, wood-frame architecture of Katsura (which has influenced so many

1. *Aerial view looking north*
2. *Entry-level floor plan*
3. *Golf-level floor plan*
4. *Entrance facade*

1

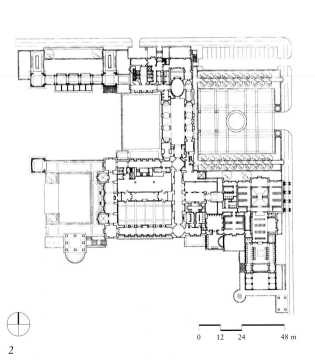

2

0   12   24   48 m

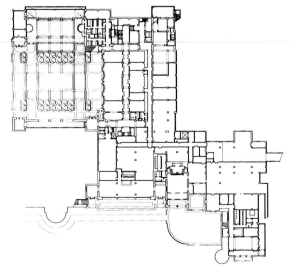

3

5

American architects, particularly those working at the scale of the house) but the less well-known masonry architecture of the Horyu-ji Temple complex (552–645) in Nara and the Osaka Castle (1586).

The focus of our building is a reflecting pool framed on three sides that opens on the west to a view of mountains. The pool provides a central, visually dominating but inaccessible place. This idea, borrowed from the architecture of traditional Japanese Zen gardens (as in Ryoan-ji), provides a tranquil counterpoint architecturally as well as for guests as they move from one activity to another within the resort. Garden pavilions extend the building into the landscape and create outdoor rooms. The Golf Academy, situated to the north of the main building, continues the same architectural language and relationship to the landscape.

5. *Elevator tower seen across reflecting pool*
6. *Lower garden*
7. *Motor court entrance*
8. *View of elevator tower from Golf Academy*

73

7

8

9. Golfers' gallery
10. Lobby
11 (overleaf). View across reflecting pool to lower garden
12 (overleaf). South facade with golfer's grill room below and banquet gallery above

11, 12

Residence in the Midwestern United States

1990–1992

The long, low, rambling mass of this house was inspired by the Shingle style; the design also pays homage to the local Greek Revival vernacular with a Doric colonnade that gives the principal covered porch a dignity in keeping with its commanding position overlooking the meadow and ponds below. The linearly organized plan provides an open gallery leading past a double-height, barrel-vaulted living hall and dining room to the family room. Beyond lie the owners' private quarters, consisting of a library and master-bedroom suite. The several skewed "legs" of the plan, devised to articulate the enfilade in relation to functional requirements, come together in the combined family room/kitchen, at once the physical and social center of the house.

1. Site plan
2. South facade

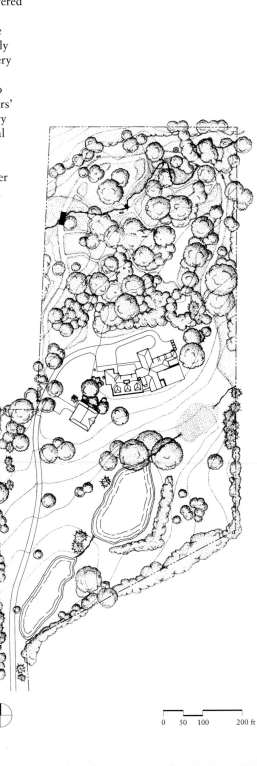

0   50   100   200 ft

1

3

4

3. Porch
4. Entrance (north) facade
5. First-floor plan
6. Second-floor plan

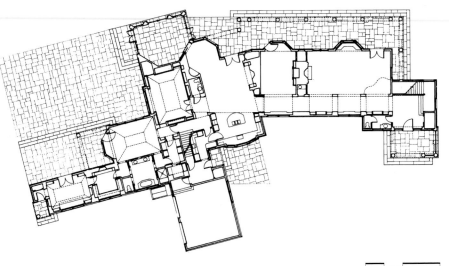

5

0   8   16   32 ft

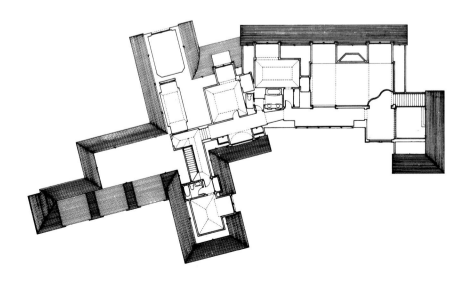

7. *Family-room inglenook*
8. *Gallery*
9. *Stairway and gallery*
10. *View of living room from balcony*

7

8

9

Brooklyn Law School

Brooklyn, New York
1990–1994

1. *Fourth-floor student dining terrace*
2. *Site plan*
3. *View from northeast*

84   Our campanile-like tower provides the ninety-year-old Brooklyn Law School with expanded facilities and an image more appropriate to its long history and growing reputation. It also tackles a difficult contextual problem. An addition to an embarrassingly ugly, banal, but much larger building of the 1960s that must continue as the law school's "main" building and front door, the new tower was intended—and has succeeded—as the school's architectural symbol. This institutional signature is also visually connected to the various classical buildings serving the courts and other government agencies in Brooklyn's civic center.

1

2

4. *Fifth-floor
(classroom) plan*
5. *Second-floor
(library) plan*
6. *Ground-floor plan*
7. *Student dining room*

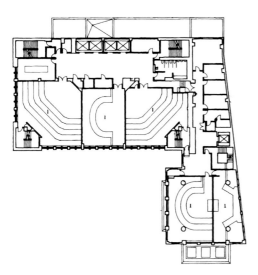

4

5

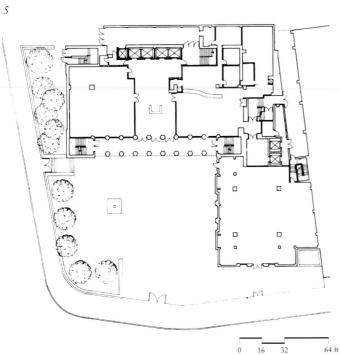

0   16   32   64 ft

6

8. *View toward periodical room*
9. *Reserve reading room*
10. *Reserve reading room*
11. *Faculty library*

88

8

9

10

Celebration

Celebration, Florida
1987–1997

90 When fully developed, Celebration, encompassing 4,900 acres, will be home to about 20,000 people. Planned in partnership with Cooper, Robertson & Partners, it demonstrates the continuing validity of traditional American town planning. A network of pedestrian-friendly streets and alleyways combined with a series of linked perimeter parks define residential neighborhoods focused on a downtown core that groups civic buildings, office buildings, shops, and apartments. The golf course, commonly privatized in recent subdivisions, is here bordered by a public street that transforms it from a single-purpose facility into a parklike amenity to be enjoyed by all. Approximately five hundred houses and apartments as well as almost half of the projected downtown are now built, as well as a program-matically innovative medical facility, Celebration Health (see p. 194), designed by this office.

1. *Aerial view*
2. *Aerial view*
3. *Aerial view*

1

2

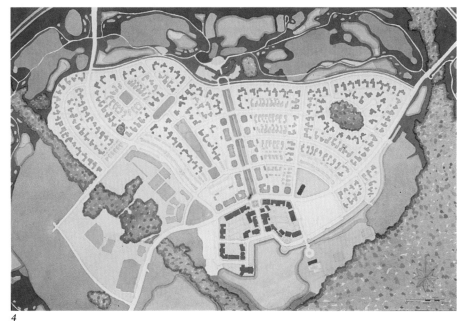

4

5

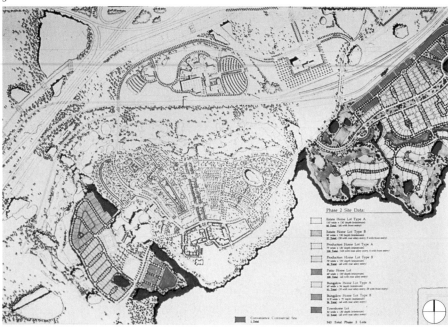

6

Taking cues from traditional Southern towns such as Beaufort, South Carolina, downtown Celebration is focused on a new lake that overlooks the existing wooded wetlands, creating an intimate relationship between the town and nature. Residential neighborhoods radiate out from this center in a warped grid plan that allows for easy visitor orientation while creating picturesque views down curved streets. Streets always terminate in parks, waterways, or natural woodlands. Garages are located on alleys, opening the streets to views of houses rather than of garage doors. At the same time the alleys act as important social condensers, fostering exchange between residents of considerably different economic groups—a key part of a larger strategy that calls for a variety of house sizes and prices in order to accommodate the demographic variety typical of towns as opposed to the economically stratified homogeneity of tract developments. Houses are designed according to the town's Residential Architectural Guidelines, prepared by the town planners in conjunction with the firm UDA, to ensure an appropriately Southern character.

In addition to master planning and overall architectural review, which we shared with Cooper, Robertson, our firm was responsible for the detailed architectural design of eleven buildings in the downtown, incorporating 123 apartments and 150,000 square feet of retail, entertainment, and office space.

4. *Village plan*
5. *Land-use plan*
6. *Phase II plan*
7. *Town-center building with restaurants and apartments*
8. *Town-center courtyard*

7

8

9. Restaurant
10. Dining porch at restaurant
11. View along Market Street
12 (overleaf). Town center

94

9

10

11

Residence in Starwood

Aspen, Colorado
1991–1996

98 Located on the side of Red Mountain just outside Aspen, enjoying spectacular views of the Roaring Fork Valley and the ski slopes at Aspen and Snowmass, this house is organized on three floors with the entrance and principal rooms at the middle level and bedrooms on the floor above. The lower floor contains athletic facilities, including an indoor pool and a racquetball court. Living areas are situated along the west front to take advantage of light and view, while service areas are set into the hill.

The exterior composition of projecting pavilions and bays arranged around a central cubic volume reduces the apparent mass of the house. Exterior tawny granite walls, a mottled purple and green slate roof, and natural wood trim help the house blend into its setting, but rigorous geometry and strong lines of symmetry carved into the south garden court dispel any false sense of camouflage.

1

1. North facade
2. Site plan
3. View from southwest

2

0   25   50   100 ft

4

4. *South facade*
5. *South terrace*
6. *Porch*

6

7

8

7. Entrance hall
8. Porch fireplace
9. Ground-floor plan
10. Living room looking toward library
11. First-floor plan
12. Second-floor plan
13 (overleaf). Indoor pool

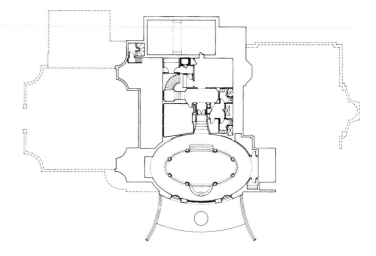

0   10 20   40 ft

9

10

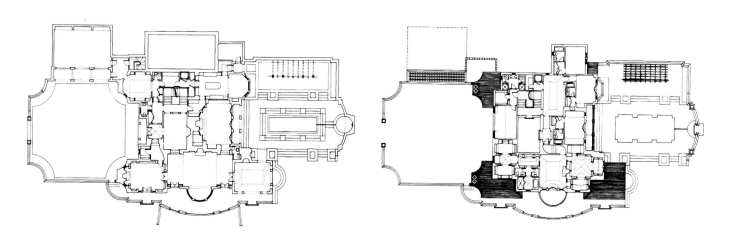

Feature Animation Building, The Walt Disney Company

Burbank, California
1991–1994

Animation is the core business and spiritual heart of the Disney enterprise. So the design of the first new building for this division since the Burbank studio was built in 1939–1940 was not undertaken lightly. For almost ten years, Disney's animators had been flourishing in seven cramped, chaotic warehouse-studios scattered through Glendale and Burbank. Fearing that a united facility would stifle creativity, Disney's administration had resisted a new building. In fact, in his instructions to us, Michael Eisner asked that what he called the "creative clutter" of our own office/studio be reflected in the new building.

The 240,000-square-foot Animation Building, housing over 700 employees, occupies a highly visible site between Disney's Burbank studio lot and the Ventura Freeway; in fact, Walt Disney first proposed to build Disneyland on this site. Given animation's critical importance to the company's identity and soul, it was essential that the new building transcend its program and become a symbolic representation of its persona, an entertaining landmark of one of the world's leading providers of entertainment.

1. *Exploded axonometric, with (from top) roof, preproduction floor, production floor, postproduction/special effects floor, lower level*
2. *Ground-floor plan*
3. *View from Riverside Drive looking south*
4. *View from Griffith Park looking north*

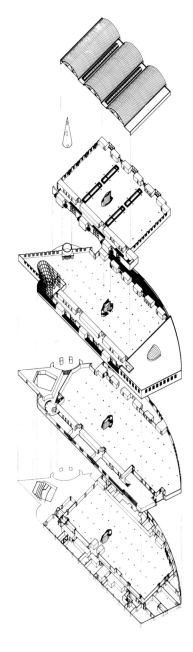

1

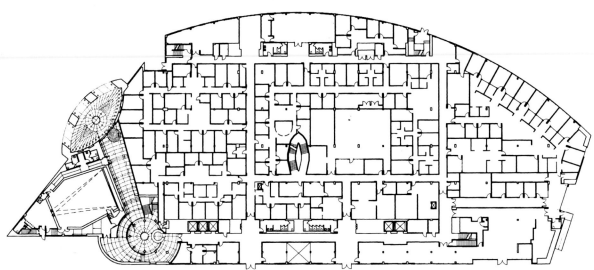

2

0   16   32   64 ft

3, 4

5

The bold shape grew out of height restrictions imposed on the site, which is bounded not only by the studio and the freeway but also by Griffith Park and a neighborhood of modest homes. The design combines Disney-based iconography, boldly scaled to be easily understood from the freeway, with a deep contextualism that connects the new supersized facility with the far smaller buildings of Kem Weber's campuslike studio across the street, especially the original Animation Building, now used for offices. Entered under a cone-shaped tower, a reference to the hat Mickey Mouse wore in his classic role as the sorcerer's apprentice but in this case the office of Roy Disney, the building reveals itself cinematically. A sequence of spaces leads past a grand triple-height light-flooded lobby and a screening room through broad circulation esplanades and top-lit crosswalks to the cavernous barrel-vaulted studios, mirroring in their form the sound stages of the studio across the way.

5. *Entrance loggia*
6. *Entrance gallery*
7. *Story room*
8. *Rotunda*

6

7

9. *Third-floor preproduction offices*
10. *Third-floor corridors*
11. *Main stairs looking up to vaulted third-floor ceiling*

9

10

112

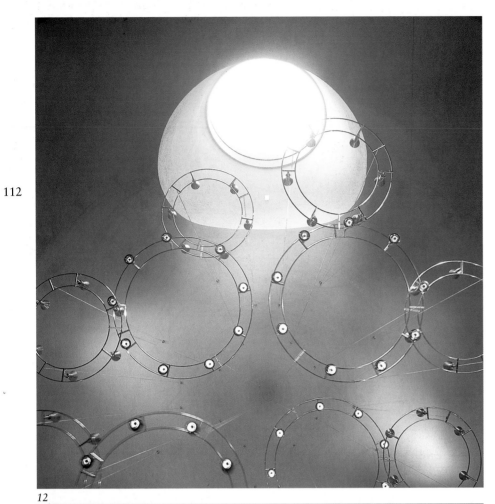

12

13

Colgate Darden
School of Business,
University of Virginia

Charlottesville, Virginia
1992–1996

116 In its architectural expression the new Darden School is based on the buildings of Thomas Jefferson, the definition of Virginia's architectural persona. The new campus is set, acropolis-like, atop the natural crest of its twenty-acre site. It is anchored by a central commons building and flanked by matching ranges of academic and faculty pavilions to the south and by a library and future auditorium with executive dining rooms to the north. Sand-struck Virginia red-brick walls with detailing of white-painted wood and limestone rise to red, painted-metal roofs. The campus mirrors the villagelike scale and character of the University of Virginia; like Jefferson's "academical village," the buildings are at once separate yet interlocked for convenience, efficiency, and sense of community.

At the heart of the new Darden campus, Saunders Hall, the commons building, contains a suite of generously proportioned reception rooms on its main level. These provide for informal student and faculty gatherings, formal meetings and receptions, and the requirements of a student café and the traditional daily Darden "coffee hour." To the south, Saunders is connected by all-weather arcades to a two-story faculty office building and, past the café and mail boxes, to a classroom building with clustered study-group rooms. Together, the commons, faculty, and classroom buildings define an academic quadrangle whose broad greensward rises gently toward an open, southern view. To the north of Saunders, a library quadrangle is framed by the three-story library building to the east and a future auditorium and executive dining building to the west.

1. *View of entry boulevard at east, with Faculty Office Building (left), Saunders Hall (center), and Camp Library (right)*
2. *Flagler Court facing Saunders Hall*

1

2

3

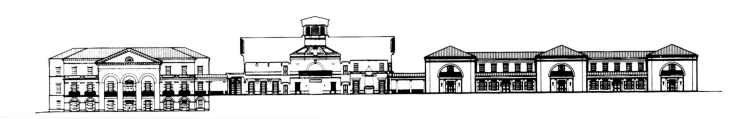

4

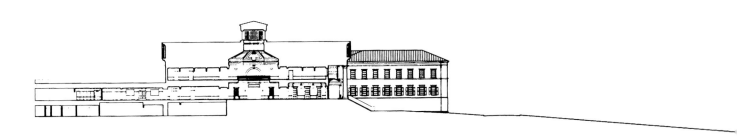

5

119

6

3. *Classroom Building Memorial Garden*
4. *Section facing east*
5. *Section facing north*
6. *Wilkinson Courtyard facing Saunders Hall (center) with Camp Library at left*
7. *Site plan*

0 20 40   80 ft

7

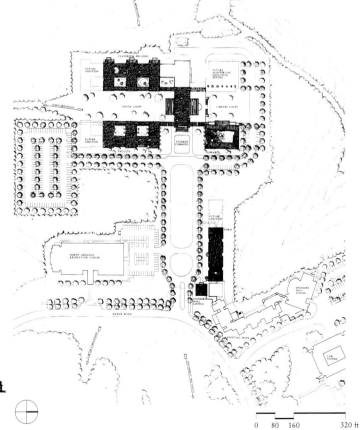

0 80 160   320 ft

8. *Camp Library reference room*
9. *First-floor plan*
10. *PepsiCo Forum in Saunders Hall*

8

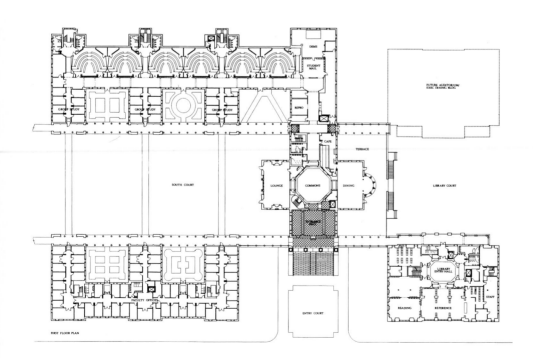

9

0 20 40   80 ft

11

122

12

13

14

Red Oaks

Cohasset, Massachusetts
1992–1996

1. *Second-floor plan*
2. *First-floor plan*
3. *Site plan*
4. *View from harbor*

124 An extensive renovation to a 1906 house perched high on a forty-foot granite outcropping overlooking Little Harbor, Red Oaks is intended to bring out the essential character of the original house by removing late additions, clarifying the plan, and adding details that were typical of houses from the era but were not evident here. A complex work of invention and reinvention, to the visitor who doesn't know its history our design looks as if a grand old house had been freshened up by new owners. In fact, that's just the effect we had in mind.

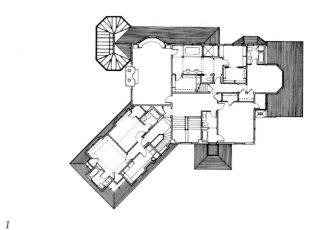

1

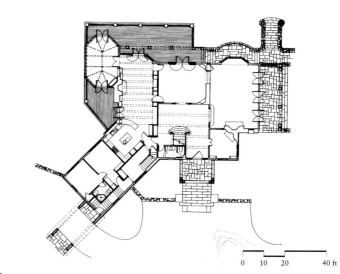

2

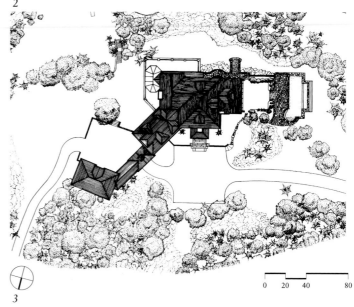

3

5

127

7

8

9. Dining room
10. Study
11. Kitchen
12. Entrance hall looking toward living room
13. Master bedroom

9

10

11

12

13

Nanki-Shirahama
Golf Clubhouse

Wakayama Prefecture, Japan
1992

1. First-floor plan
2. Site plan
3. View of dining pavilion from eighteenth green
4. View of dining pavilion across entrance courtyard

130   The natural beauty of Shirahama's rugged coastline, hilly terrain, and neighboring beaches and coves, so far from a typical Westerner's view of Japan, suggests the Amalfi coast of Italy. In keeping with this feeling, our design was inspired by ancient Roman villas, with elemental shapes defining private courtyards that open to spectacular views.

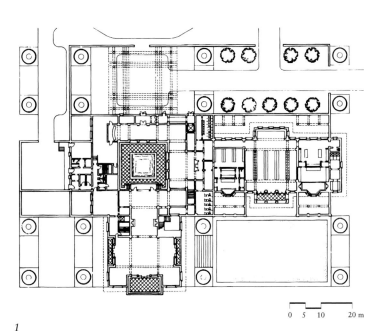

0   5   10   20 m

1

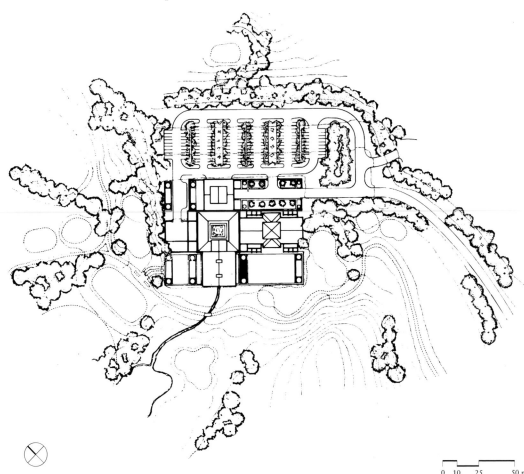

0   10   25   50 m

2

3

ANDREW ZEGA, DEL.

4

Gap Embarcadero Building

San Francisco, California
1992–2000

132   Architecture requires patience. In 1992 the Gap selected us as architects for its Embarcadero Building, located on a key San Francisco waterfront site south of Market Street. Our initial design called for a six-story base with a fifteen-story superstructure articulated as a cubic background mass and a slender foreground tower at the south, which would work together as one. The coupling of the base and the boldly scaled tower took its cues from the nearby Ferry Terminal Building: the lantern would suggest a lighthouse, and the red brick, limestone, and cast-stone facades would blend with the area's traditional warehouse character.

The slow economy and other factors put the project on hold until 1995, when the decision by CALTRANS not to rebuild the earthquake-damaged freeway ramp edging the site made it possible to increase the site area and expand the proposed building to the north. At the same time the possibility of a major financial-services company becoming a lead tenant revived hopes for realizing the project. So we redesigned the building with the base reduced by one floor and the tower relocated to the north side of the lot to make room for a high-ceilinged, column-free trading floor.

When the tenant did not sign on, the project was revisited once again with the tower relocated to the center of the building. As the design has developed it has incorporated a variety of features that promise to make the building an exemplar of environmentally responsible design. These include the use of operable windows, raised floors with underfloor air supply, double-height spaces on each floor that allow natural light to penetrate into deep interior floor areas, and fuel cells that both generate uninterrupted computer power and produce hot water with otherwise wasted heat. Construction is scheduled to begin in late 1998.

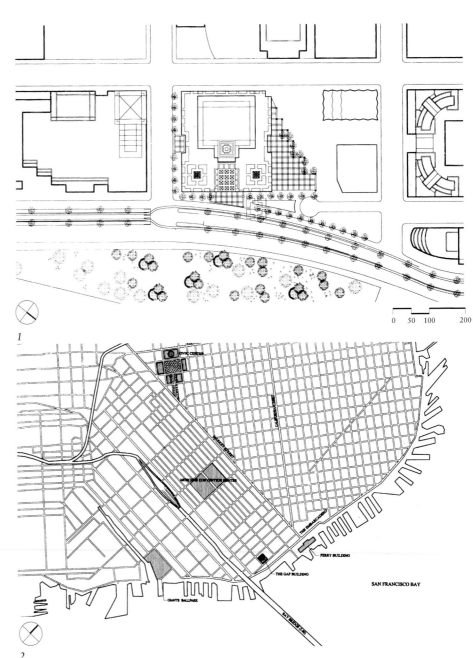

1

2

133

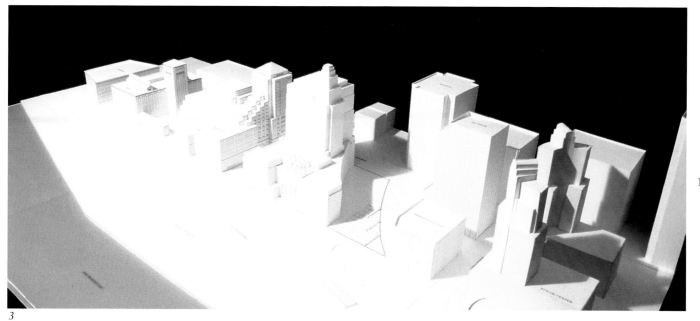

3

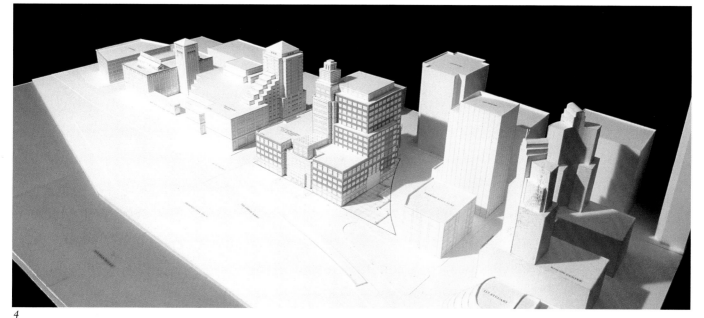

4

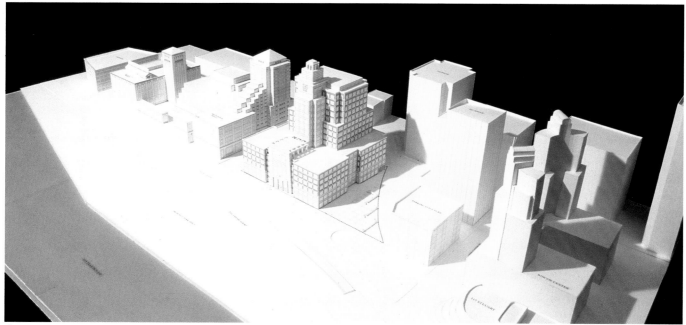

5

6

6. *Photomontage showing
   view from the Embarcadero*
7. *Ground-floor plan*
8. *Eighth-floor plan*
9. *Eleventh-floor plan*
10. *Fifteenth-floor plan*

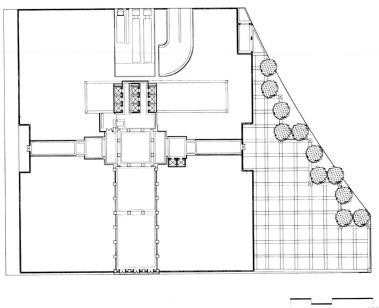

0   25   50   100 ft

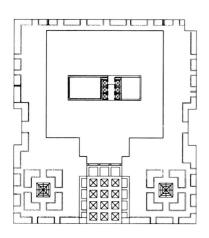

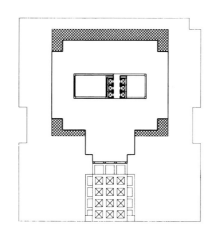

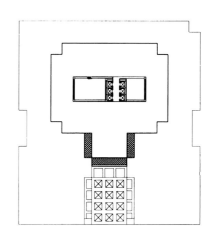

8

9

10

Residence

Kings Point, New York
1992–1997

136 A picturesque massing of shingled towers and porches was developed to reap the full benefit of what is surely one of the most spectacularly situated sites in the New York area, a commanding bluff overlooking the Long Island Sound, City Island, numerous lacy bridges, and the Manhattan skyline. The rambling composition encompasses a strictly disciplined plan of generously sized, classically proportioned and detailed rooms.

1. *Site plan*
2. *First-floor plan*
3. *Entrance (east) facade*
4. *Waterfront (west) facade*

3

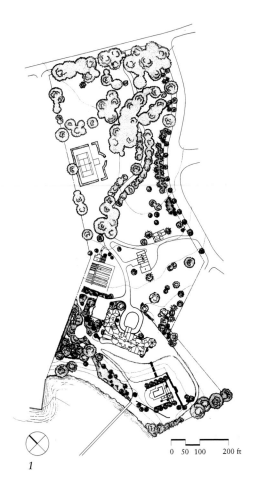

1

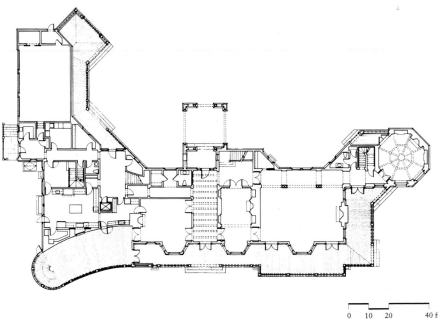

2

0   50 100   200 ft

0   10   20   40 ft

Aspen Highlands

Aspen, Colorado
1992–2001

138 In spite of some of the best expert ski terrain in North America and the greatest vertical drop of any ski area in the state of Colorado, the Highlands has suffered because of inadequate lifts and a virtually undeveloped base area. As part of an ambitious plan to help the Highlands realize its full potential, our master plan for an American alpine village at the base of the mountain contains lodge/condominium units, shops, restaurants, and skier-services facilities clustered along a sun-drenched pedestrian street. The plan, which also provides two flanking residential neighborhoods of single-family houses and townhouses, is now being implemented, with all building in the village core under our direct design control.

In its architecture, the village draws on the Western lodge tradition exemplified by such notable structures as the Ahawahnee Inn in Yosemite Valley, Old Faithful Lodge in Yellowstone Park, Timberline Lodge on Mount Hood, and Paradise Lodge on Mount Rainier. Native stone, logs, and rough clapboards form solid walls and broad eaves that shed Aspen's powdery snow and protect residents from the strong Colorado sunlight. Construction began in the summer of 1998.

1

2

1. *View of village from base of ski slope*
2. *Site plan*
3. *Perspective view of Village Square from Ski Lodge*
4. *Perspective view of Ski Lodge great room*

3

4

William Gates Computer Science Building, Stanford University

Palo Alto, California
1992–1996

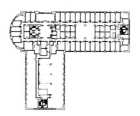
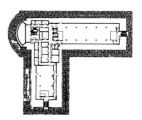

140 Like many of our buildings, this one was intended as much to meet a functional need as to help repair an urbanistic wound. The 141,000-square-foot Gates Building not only unifies the university's geographically scattered computer-research groups under a single roof; the design also serves as an important first step in a long-term plan to transform the so-called Near West portion of the campus from an expediently conceived and largely unplanned grouping of mostly dismal, utilitarian buildings into a system of academic quadrangles and walkways that extend the pattern established in Frederick Law Olmsted's original campus plan.

At the intersection of Serra Street and the north-south axis, the Gates Building has two principal entrances that reflect a basic division in the program. Facing south and opening onto Serra Street, the building's triple-height arched main entrance leads to a lobby with stairs and elevators. Facing east, an open loggia provides the building's second entrance, from which stairs lead down to a lower level where three sloped-floor auditoriums and a variety of flat-floored classrooms provide the latest in interactive and distance learning capabilities.

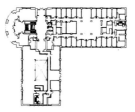
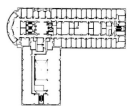

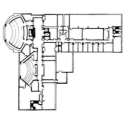
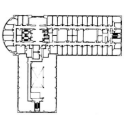

1. Second-floor, ground-floor, and basement plans
2. Fifth-, fourth-, and third-floor plans
3. Campus plan
4. View from southeast
5. View from northeast

1   *2*

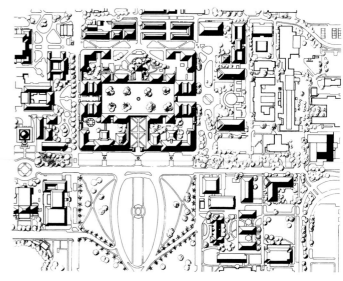

3

4, 5

6

The detailing of the Gates Building overlays warm buff limestone walls, deeply recessed windows, and low-pitched, clay tile roofs (reflecting the historic campus) on a steel frame. This frame finds its visible expression in the steel window wall that allows for natural ventilation of the interior.

While at work on the building, we were one of three firms invited to develop a master-plan concept for the Near West Campus, one that would be not only in the spirit of Olmsted's master plan, but also responsive to many of the post–World War II buildings that had to be retained, no matter their artistic limitations. Our proposal, which was not accepted, met the requirement for four new buildings, totaling 350,000 square feet, and an extensive program of site work. A proposed quadrangle echoed but did not repeat the spatial characteristics of Memorial Quadrangle of 1884–1888.

6. *Entrance lobby*
7. *Main stair*
8. *Library*
9. *Main stair and skylight*
10 *(overleaf). Faculty lounge terrace*

7

8

146

11

12

13

11. *View of mall looking south,
Near West Campus proposal*
12. *Aerial view showing relationship of
Near West Campus to main campus*
13. *Elevation looking north along Serra
Mall, Near West Campus proposal*
14. *Ground-floor plan, Near
West Campus proposal*

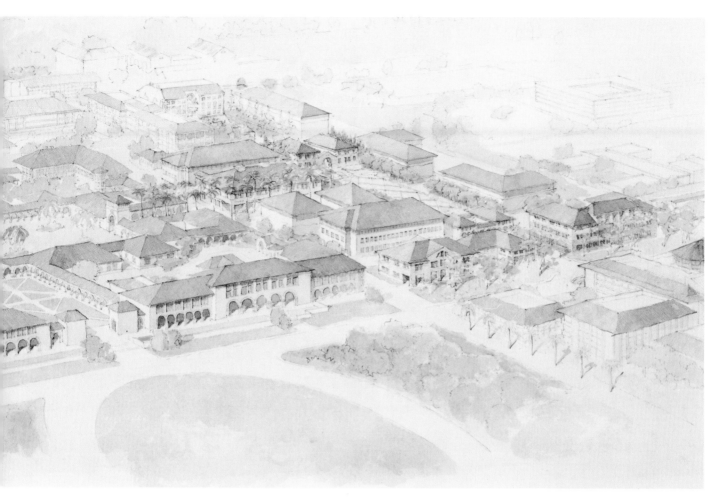

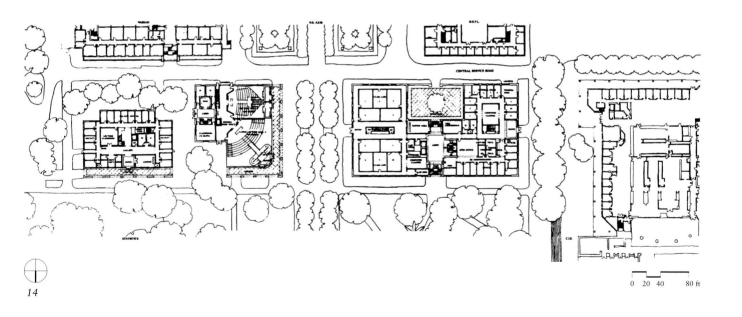

0 20 40   80 ft

Residence at Skimhampton

East Hampton, New York
1992–1993

1. *First-floor plan*
2. *Existing house*
3. *Screened porch*
4. *West facade*
5. *East facade*

148   To add onto a 1970s modernist box of no particular distinction was a serious challenge to the contextualism that has been one of the guiding principles of our work. But going "modern" was the right thing to do, and the new wing set at right angles to the rear of the original house and the screened porch attached to the front together transformed the house without sacrificing its essential character.

2

0   5   10   20 ft

1

3

4, 5

Residence

Telluride, Colorado
1992

150   For a secluded slope just outside of
town, this two-and-a-half-story house
was planned as a compound of buildings
casually arranged around a central court.
Beige stucco walls, native stone, and
natural wood complement the colors
of the surrounding semiarid landscape.

1. *Second-floor plan*
2. *First-floor plan*
3. *Site plan*
4. *View from southwest*
5. *View of entry court*

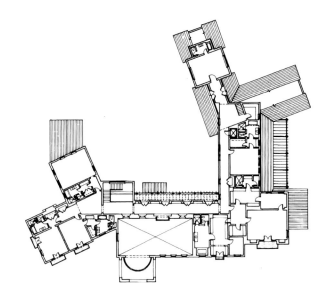

1

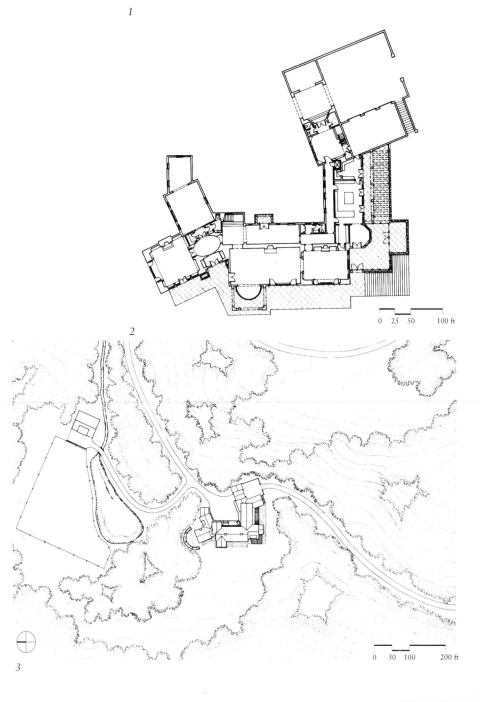

2

0   25   50   100 ft

3

0   50   100   200 ft

4

5

Residence in Beverly Park

Beverly Hills, California
1993–1994

152   This unrealized project was for a large site in a new subdivision. The flat land, bereft of landscaping, looked very much like Beverly Hills and Bel Air looked in the 1920s and 1930s when they too were new places and architects like Wallace Neff were inspired to appropriate the traditional architecture of another dry landscape, that of southern Spain, in particular the *fincas* and *cortijos* of Andalusia and Mallorca.

Nourished by Neff's example and by a trip to southern Spain, we set to work grouping areas of the large house into distinct pavilions around a series of courts and gardens punctuated by fountains and connected with rills. We hoped that the house in time might not only become one with the landscape but also capitalize on the possibilities of outdoor living that California's benign climate promises but that, in our air-conditioned world, are seldom exploited.

1

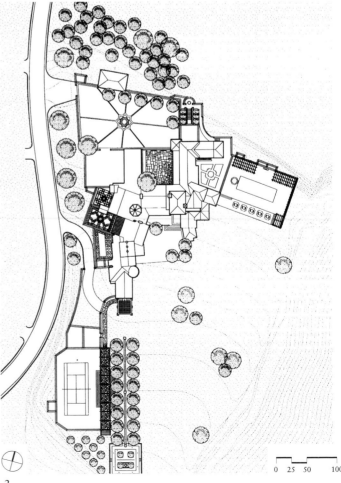

2

1. *View from south*
2. *Site plan*
3. *First floor plan*

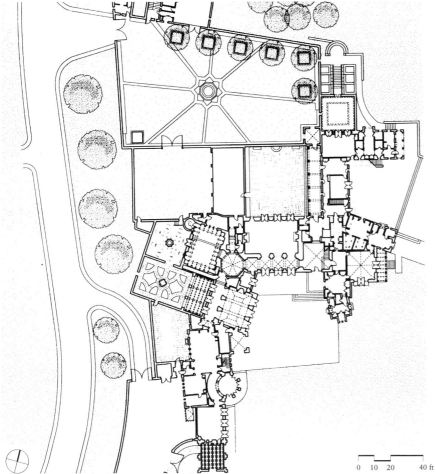

0 10 20   40 ft

3

Additions to Points of View

Seal Harbor, Maine
1992–1993

The only thing that approaches the pleasure an architect gets in being asked to design a new building is that of being asked back when new work needs to be done on one from his or her past. Points of View, completed in 1976, was the first serious step in the progression of Shingle-style houses that it has been my reward to follow for over twenty years. I saw the invitation to add a study and new screened porch (to replace a covered porch since closed in) as an opportunity to correct defects in the original design— the awkward entrance caused by its downhill location and the somewhat boxlike massing. In the update, we reconfigured the front entrance, positioning it at the midpoint of the stairway to create a better, and inside a more dramatic, point of arrival. The new screened porch, with its curving arc partially bermed in, achieves an embracing expansiveness that at last addresses the site with an appropriate gesture.

We also added an English squash court, standard and candlepin bowling lanes, and changing rooms to an existing squash house. The bowling alley, 130 feet long, has a one-and-a-half-story circular seating area at its west end. This towerlike end-piece defines a new entry court carved out of the pine woods.

1

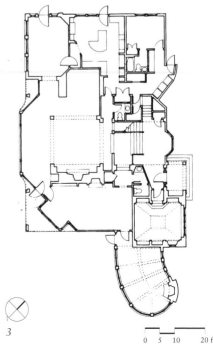

2

1. *View from southwest*
2. *View of original house from east*
3. *Ground-floor plan*
4. *View from southeast*

3

0 5 10   20 ft

4

5

7. *View of playhouse from northwest*
8. *Twilight view of bowling-alley wing of playhouse from north*
9. *Sitting area in bowling alley*

158

7

8

42nd Street Now!

New York, New York
1992–2001

1. *North side of Forty-second Street*
in the 1970s
2. *Rendering of redevelopment concept*
illustrating globe icon at the "crossroads
of the world" site

160 By the late 1970s, the theater block of
Forty-second Street, once the symbolic
heart of the Big Apple's entertainment
district, had become rotten to the core.
In 1987 we developed guidelines for
the adaptive reuse of five theaters on
the block. But plans for the revitalization
of the theaters, tied to the development
of four supersized office buildings at
the Times Square end of the block
traditionally known as the "crossroads
of the world," were stalled by lawsuits
and by the deep economic recession of
the early 1990s.

In 1992, in order to jump-start the street's
revitalization, the city and state agencies
working together as the 42nd Street
Development Corporation Inc. invited
our team of architects and designers to
provide an interim plan for the block,
which in its abandoned condition had
become an embarrassingly visible symbol
of New York's decline. Our plan included
proposed uses for the lower floors of
currently vacated or underutilized sites
and, as a critical step toward getting
things moving, the development of a
forward-looking image based on, but not
tied to, Forty-second Street's past. Our
plan was governed by six principles:
layering, unplanning, contradiction and
surprise, pedestrian experience, visual
anchors, and aesthetics as attractions.
We proposed returning the street to
its traditional role as an entertainment
center, with new signs and lights over-
laying what was already in place, adding
new dimensions to what was an almost
archaeological record of twentieth-century
New York's architectural and entertainment history. Most importantly, our plan
insisted on treating the entire block as a
single entity, with strong architecture and
uses anchoring its Seventh and Eighth
Avenue corners. We would thereby over-
come a weakness that had plagued the
block through the century when Eighth
Avenue was first given over to burlesque
and prostitution and later to the block-
buster scale of a bus station.

1

3. Forty-second Street, 1993
4. Forty-second Street, 1997

3

164   Timing is everything in architecture, as in most things. For a decade or more the Forty-second Street project had been pilloried by the press and ignored by the entertainment industry. But just as work on our deeply contextual plan, accompanied by strong and believable imagery showing how the reborn street might look, was nearing completion, the Walt Disney Company began to look for a theater to house a new corporate venture: musical plays. Once Disney agreed to take over the architecturally distinguished but disastrously decayed New Amsterdam Theater, the largest theater on the block, other entertainment companies took notice and began to vie for spots on the born-again street. In response to interest in the Eighth Avenue end of the block, we prepared a set of guidelines for a retail, entertainment, and hotel complex; these were used to sponsor a competition that led to the selection of a bold design, demonstrating that new large-scale construction need not be dull. We also designed a temporary storefront exhibition as a way of introducing the public and developers to Forty-second Street's rich history and current opportunities.

In 1996 the reborn street began to take shape when portions of the plan and the detailed use and signage guidelines were implemented on an interim basis, in the partial restoration of the historic Rialto Building and the construction of a temporary Disney store. Overnight, it seemed, bleakness gave way to a blaze of signs and lights, mixing traditional and new technologies with historic and new buildings. We are particularly proud of our work on this project. Forty-second Street is reborn but remains true to its nature: it is once again secure as New York's premier democratic entertainment center and is also a widely studied model for urban redevelopment worldwide.

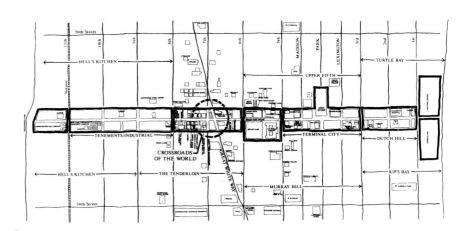

5

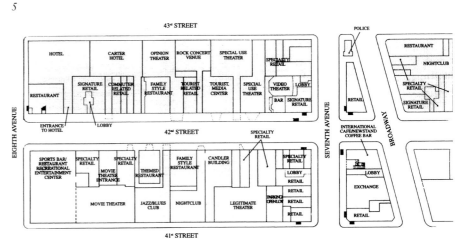

6

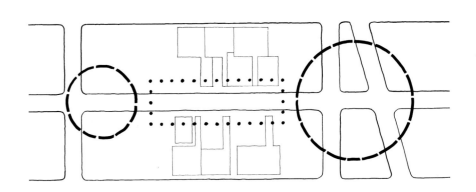

7

0   50   100   200 ft

8

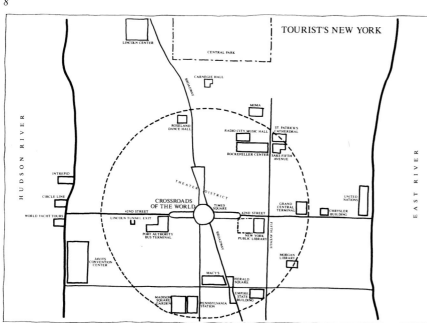

TOURIST'S NEW YORK

9

10

11

10. 42nd Street Now! exhibit and Times Square Business Improvement District information desk
11. Entrance to 42nd Street Now! exhibit
12. Massing requirements
13. Sample massing
14. Guideline study model for the northeast corner of Eighth Avenue and Forty-second Street

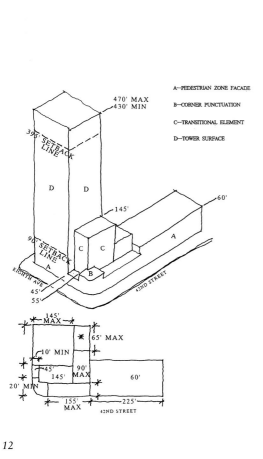

A—PEDESTRIAN ZONE FACADE
B—CORNER PUNCTUATION
C—TRANSITIONAL ELEMENT
D—TOWER SURFACE

12

14

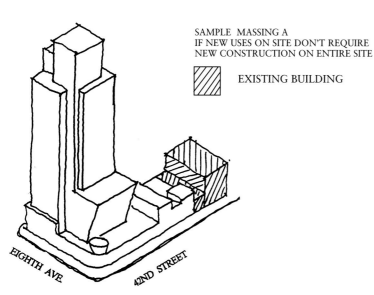

SAMPLE MASSING A
IF NEW USES ON SITE DON'T REQUIRE NEW CONSTRUCTION ON ENTIRE SITE

EXISTING BUILDING

13

15

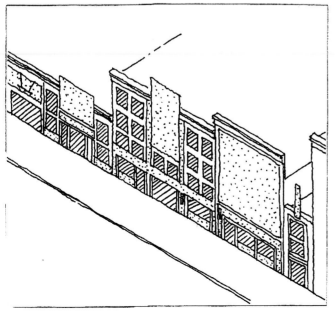

16

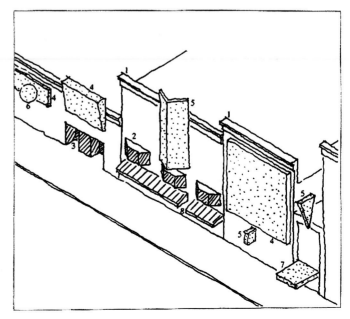

17

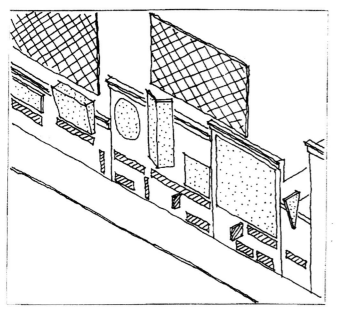

18

19

15. North side of Forty-second Street near Eighth Avenue, 1993
16. Guideline diagram showing facade dominated by windows and commercial signs
17. Guideline diagram showing three-dimensional elements on facade
18. Forty-second Street and Seventh Avenue, fall 1997 at Disney corner
19. Guideline diagram showing storefront signage, business signage, and commercial signage

East Hampton Library

East Hampton, New York
1992–1997

170   During the course of the twentieth century, the East Hampton Library, the core of which was built in 1910, has been much enlarged to accommodate a growing community and expanding collections. But the additions were somewhat ad hoc, leaving dead ends. Moreover, with no new work on the building since 1975, the library was virtually overwhelmed by the information technology that has become a key part of learning in the past ten years. While meeting the needs of present technology and endeavoring to anticipate future trends in this area, we have nonetheless continued the Tudorbethan style of the historic library, reinvigorating what by the time of the last addition had become quite watery. Two new intersecting wings make circulation within the library continuous while creating a quiet outdoor space for children's storytelling. Though our detailing is more robust than that of many of the additions, we were careful not to upstage Aymar Embury II's original building, which remains the showpiece.

1. Site plan
2. West facade
3. Courtyard
4. Main Street facade

2

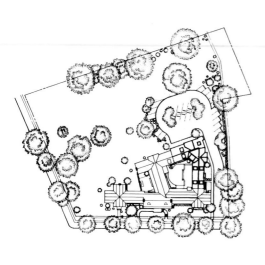

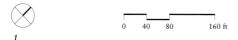

1

0   40   80   160 ft

3

172

5

6

7

5. Entry
6. Reading alcove
7. Stair to lower level
8. Ground-floor plan
9. Fiction collection

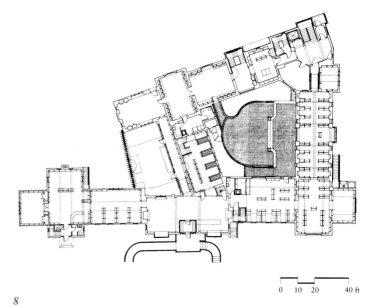

8

0 10 20   40 ft

Hotel Melayu

Kuala Lumpur, Malaysia
1992

1. *View of guest-room pavilions and garden*
2. *Entry-level plan*
3. *Dining-room courtyard*
4. *Elevation*

174   Intended for a site in the heart of the city next to a traditionally designed complex of museums devoted to showcasing the diverse cultures of Malaysia, our proposal for the Hotel Melayu complements its neighbor with a design reflecting traditional village scale and architectural character.

1

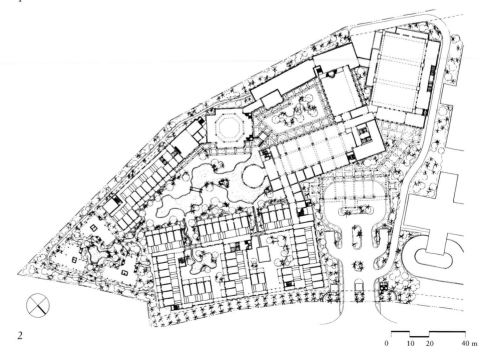

2

0 10 20   40 m

3

0 5 10   20 m

4

Moore Psychology Building, Dartmouth College

Hanover, New Hampshire
1992–1999

176 In a departure from the situation we often work in, where a new building is inserted into an established setting, Moore Hall, in a new part of the campus, is the standard-bearer for our client's renewed respect for its own traditional white-trimmed, red-brick architecture. The site is part of a new north campus quadrangle that may or may not be realized; our building will either remain a "stand-alone" or become a piece of infill. In other words, this is a contextual building awaiting its context.

While the intent of many at the college was to have a building that says "Dartmouth," there were some who were anxious that it say so in a distinctly modern way. This was an understandable point given that most of Dartmouth's Georgian and Georgian Revival buildings are residential in scale and Moore Hall, filled with laboratories and other special facilities requiring big spaces with high ceilings, was surely of a different magnitude. This is not to say that Dartmouth has no other large-scale buildings, including laboratory buildings, but that their designs have tended to be self-referential, and in some cases self-important, perhaps saying something about art or science but remaining silent about Dartmouth's traditions. With all this in mind, plus a healthy respect for the rigors of Hanover's winter climate—which must be respected in selecting and shaping materials and details—we designed a granite-and-limestone-trimmed red-brick building like so many others at Dartmouth but with its own distinct size, scale, and personality: a member of the college family but also a unique individual and definitely not a clone.

1. *Site plan with existing conditions*
2. *New building in relation to proposed master plan*
3. *Basement plan*
4. *Ground-floor plan*
5. *Perspective view from street*
6. *Perspective view from proposed quadrangle*

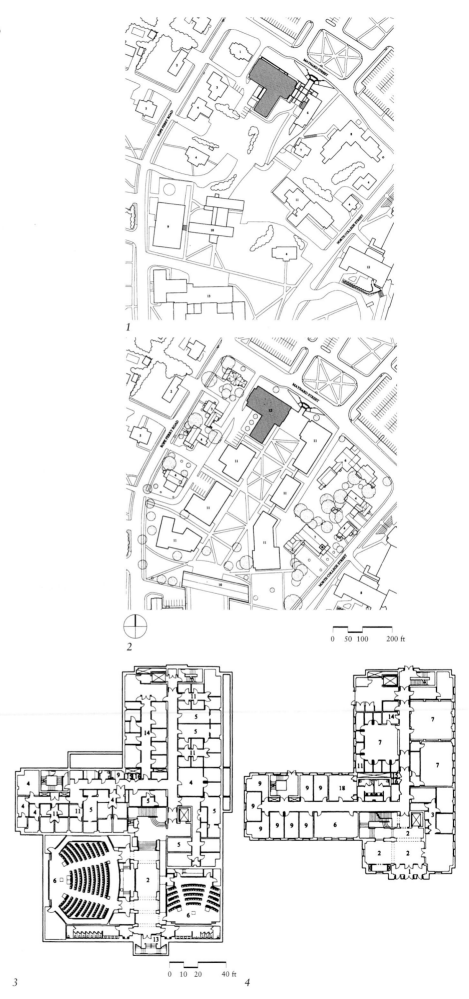

5

6

Disney's BoardWalk

Walt Disney World,
Lake Buena Vista, Florida
1993–1996

178 The BoardWalk joins our previously built
Disney Yacht and Beach Club Hotels to
complete a lakeside resort district with
a unity of vision comparable to that of
the Swan and Dolphin Hotels to its west
and to that of Epcot, immediately to its
east. Functionally two hotels sharing a
common lobby and convention facility,
the BoardWalk is a large project, with
about one thousand guest rooms and
forty-nine thousand square feet of retail
space, designed to suggest a naturally
evolved town. The meeting facility sets
the historic style clock in motion with a
sprawling bracketed Victorian-Gothic hall
such as might have served a nineteenth-
century New England seaside community
as a social or cultural center.

1. *Site plan*
2. *Entry*
3. *County-fair-themed swimming pool*
   at the BoardWalk Villas

2

1

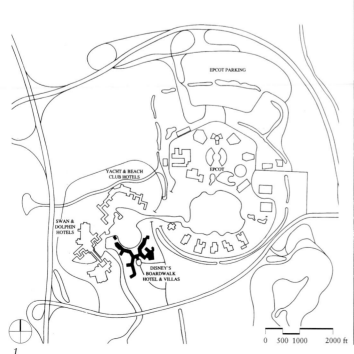

3

4

5

6

Facing Crescent Lake, the BoardWalk Inn and the BoardWalk Villas bring the style story forward in time. The inn is arranged around a series of garden courts, each distinct, including private gardens leading to duplex honeymoon cottages. It takes its architectural cue from the rambling Colonial Revival of the 1880s and 1890s. The BoardWalk Villas confront the lake with a series of interconnected, idiosyncratic, small-scale buildings. But facing the canal is a singular composition of wide roof overhangs and bold horizontals that nod to the early architecture of Frank Lloyd Wright and the Prairie Bungalow school, bringing the historical evolution of the architecture of the resort town to a conclusion that suggests the incipient modernism of the early twentieth century.

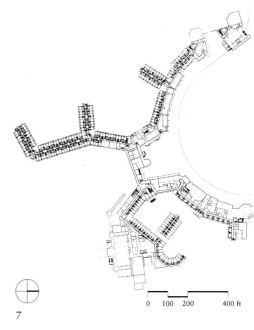

0   100   200   400 ft

7

4. *Entry porte cochere*
5. *Honeymoon cottages at BoardWalk Inn*
6. *View from lobby porch toward Crescent Lake*
7. *Ground-floor plan*
8. *Pool at BoardWalk Inn*
9. *BoardWalk Convention Center*

8

9

182

10

11

12

14

15

Residence in Preston Hollow

Dallas, Texas
1993–1999

190   On a large site overlooking a pond but otherwise bereft of landscape improvements, this brick and stone house is one of our most geometrically disciplined to date. An axial sequence leads from the motor court through the centrally located living room to the lawn on the south side of the property, where a naturalistic landscape of trees and grass leads to a flight of broad steps at the water's edge.

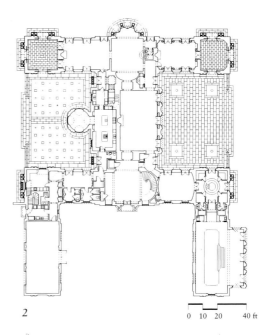

2

0 10 20   40 ft

1

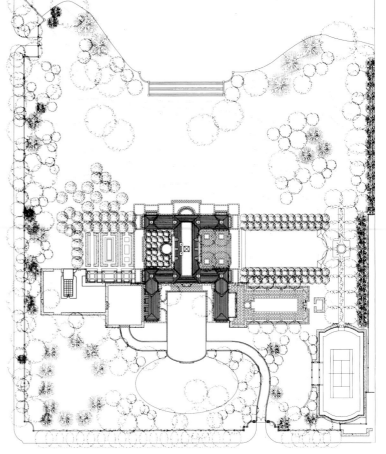

0 25 50   100 ft

1. *South facade*
2. *First-floor plan*
3. *Site plan*
4. *West elevation*
5. *North elevation*

4

5

Concert Hall and Museum

Karuizawa, Japan
1993

192 Karuizawa, Japan's oldest mountain resort, which was first colonized by the British in the eighteenth century, lies at the foot of the active volcano Mount Asama, about one hundred miles northwest of Tokyo. Intended for a heavily wooded, moss-covered, sloping, triangular, five-acre site about two miles uphill from the town center, the cultural center was to be home to Seiji Ozawa, who would conduct a master class there in the late summer. In the off-season winter months the facilities would serve the year-round residents of the town. The program, in combination with prefectural requirements relating to the existing natural landscape and to stringent height, setback, and buildable-area restrictions, prompted a site plan composed of discrete one- and two-story buildings arranged sequentially in a manner inspired by classical Greek acropolis planning. Though distinctly influenced by traditional Western forms, the various fieldstone, wood, and metal-roofed buildings, with their overhanging gable roofs, also seem comfortable within the context of traditional Japanese garden architecture.

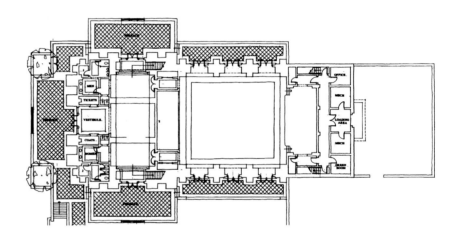

1

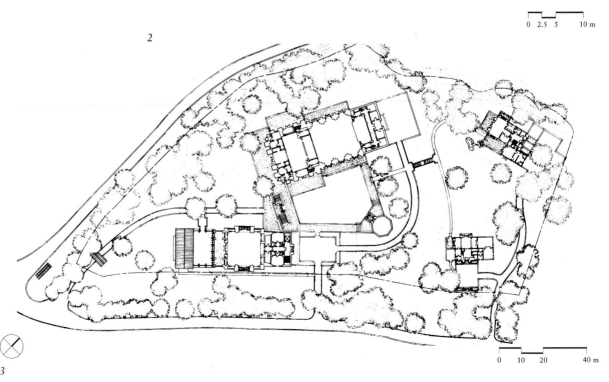

2

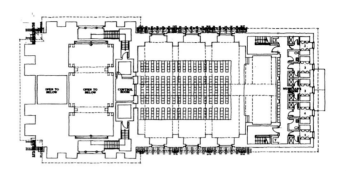

3

4

5

6

Celebration Health

Celebration, Florida
Phase I, 1993–1997
Phase II, 1996–1998

194 Florida Hospital's Celebration Health campus, reflecting some of the most inventive thinking in the health-care field, represents a pioneering mixture of traditional in- and outpatient health care with major facilities for health and physical education. The site is a sixty-five-acre campus that is an integral part of the new town of Celebration but is separated from the town center by the golf course and a limited access road. Celebration Health, building on our work in Columbus, Indiana (see p. 40), goes even further in departing from the institutional image of typical health-care facilities. Functionally expressive, informally connected pavilions designed with a familiar, regionally based vocabulary help render obvious the programmatic conviction that this facility not be perceived as a conventional hospital but as a community facility built around the idea of wellness. Low-pitched terra-cotta tile roofs, vine-covered pergolas, and cream-colored stucco walls work together with a lush central Florida landscape to create a welcoming, healing environment. Inside, a continuous galleria, off of which all departments open, provides natural light and views to departmental waiting areas, clarifying orientation within the building and helping to articulate the unorthodox variety of services offered.

1. *View from northeast, with (from left) medical office building, entry porte cochere, stair tower, fitness pavilion, chapel, and bed wing*
2. *Location plan*
3. *Site plan, phase I*
4. *Site plan, full build-out*

1

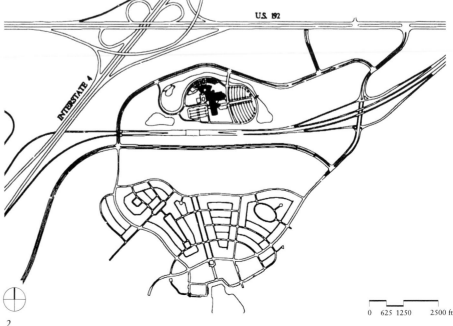

2

0   625 1250   2500 ft

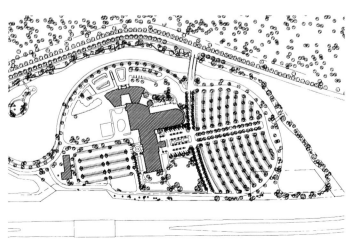
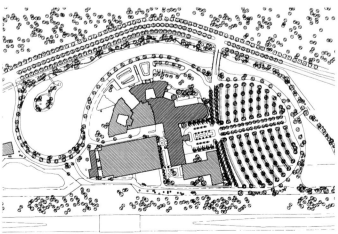

0   125   250   500 ft

196

5

6

198

8

9

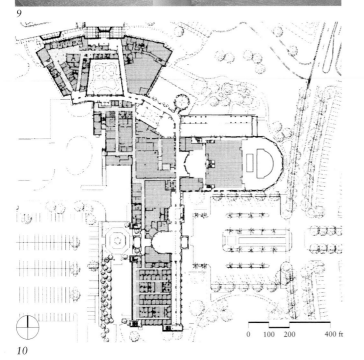

10

8. *Chapel*
9. *Swimming pool*
10. *Ground-floor plan*
11. *Main lobby*
12 *(overleaf). View from golf course*

0   100   200   400 ft

Product Design

202   Designs for glassware and flatware for Sasaki put an architectural spin on table-top objects. Traditional patterns of masonry coursing transform drinking glasses and serving bowls into crystalline buildings; abstracted campaniles make a place setting of flatware into a towered Tuscan townscape. Memories of archetypal classical motifs, such as the Greek key pattern, and the voluptuous curves of Greek vessels, such as the kylix, resonate throughout our lighting collection for Baldinger. Our work for HBF includes a club chair named for a swank nightspot of the 1930s, where glamour and comfort coincided. We have also designed a line of fabrics that outlines, in an abstract way, a grand tour of Europe, encompassing cities that are particular touchstones for our work in architecture.

1

2

4

3

5

6. *HBF London, Stockholm, and Berlin fabrics*
7. *HBF Vienna, Glasgow, and London fabrics*
8. *HBF Paris, Stockholm, and Prague fabrics*

204

6

8

7

9. Sasaki Brique vase and bowl
10. Sasaki Brique barware
11. Sasaki Torii flatware

9

11

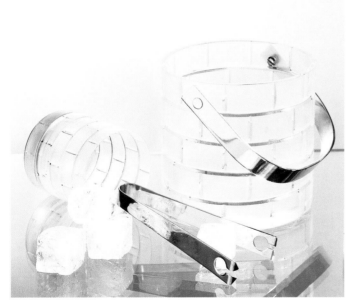

10

Residence

Montecito, California
1993–1998

206   In a sense, this house is seventy years overdue. In the mid-1920s a site was prepared for it at the top of a spectacular stepped water garden designed by Elmer Awl. The garden was built but the house was not. Much later the property was subdivided and an artificial pond was added, with some stone walls at one end that were intended to be the basement of a house, which also was not built. When we were asked to design a large house for the property, we chose to honor Awl's work with an H-shaped villa at the approximate location intended for the original house and to anchor the new pond in the larger landscape with a mostly underground pavilionlike building housing a screening room. A guest house and, at the entrance, a gardener's cottage complete the development.

Our villa sits at the northern terminus of the main axis, enabling Awl's garden at last to resolve itself; the position maximizes views east and south toward the ocean. The major rooms, commanding the garden and the court between them, initiate the formal progress downhill. Toward the east the plan relaxes as it opens to an outdoor swimming pool set on a terrace overlooking a spectacular stone pine and the valley beyond.

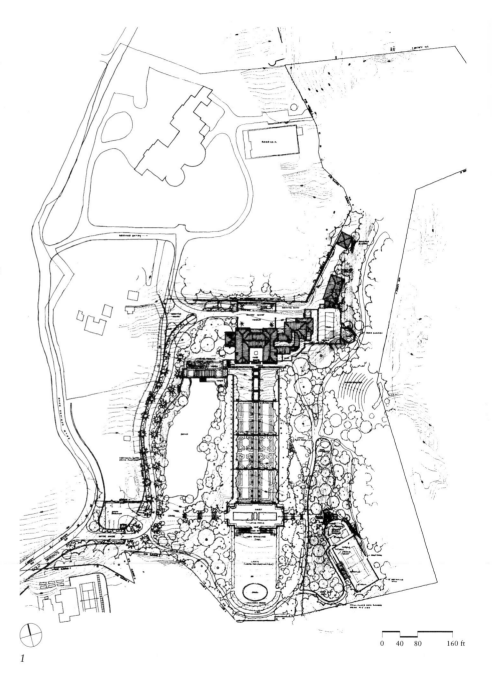

1

0   40   80   160 ft

3

4

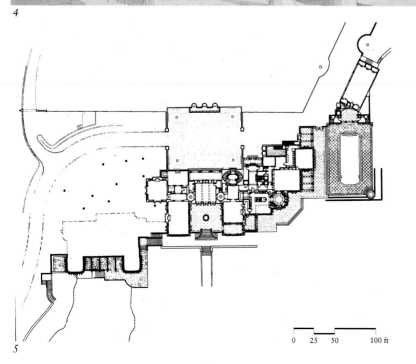

5

0   25   50   100 ft

Residence at North York

Toronto, Canada
1993–1998

210   This slate-roofed rubblestone house occupies a double lot in one of metropolitan Toronto's oldest suburbs. To take full advantage of the small site, the mass of the house shapes the outdoor space into a series of separate garden rooms. The composition of semidiscrete pavilions also reduces the apparent bulk of the house. The plan organizes a complex program around a double-height, handkerchief-vaulted, lantern-lit stair hall. As built, the house succeeds an earlier, fully developed scheme for a more elaborate house on the same site (1988–1993).

2

1

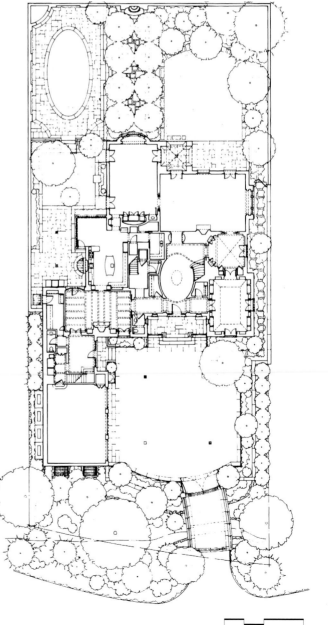

3

0   8   16   32 ft

4

5

Smith Campus Center, Pomona College

Claremont, California
1993–1999

212   Set at the intersection of the two most important campus circulation axes, the campus center replaces a 1937 facility that was subsumed in an artistically infelicitous 1970 expansion. It recaptures the site intentions of Myron Hunt's 1913 campus plan with its U-shaped building surrounding three sides of an open-air courtyard. In keeping with the master plan, covered outdoor galleries provide circulation through the building. Also in keeping with tradition, the center, like Hunt's buildings and those of his successor, Sumner Spaulding, will be built of exposed, board-formed reinforced concrete, combined with simple cast-stone detailing and industrial steel-frame windows rising to a barrel-tile roof. Construction commenced in October 1997.

1. View from College Walk Quadrangle
2. Site plan
3. Ground-floor plan

1

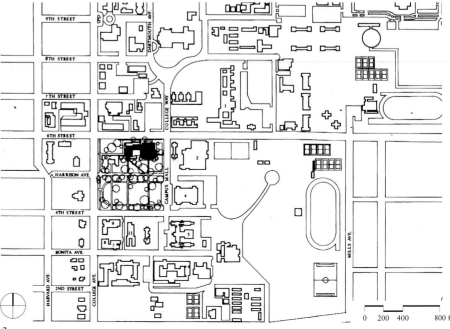

2

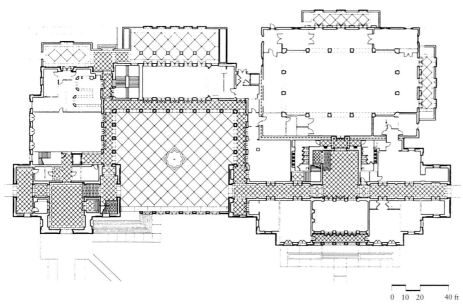

National Advocacy Center, U.S. Department of Justice, University of South Carolina

Columbia, South Carolina
1993–1998

214   Designed and built for the federal government, but located on the historic campus of the University of South Carolina, the 262,000-square-foot National Advocacy Center is a specialized training facility serving all federal legal employees but primarily the Department of Justice's nationwide corps of United States attorneys. Under an unusual but mutually beneficial arrangement, the completed building is owned by the university but leased to the Department of Justice for twenty-five years, which in turn shares portions of the center with the National District Attorneys Association. The center's program includes ten courtrooms where United States and district attorneys hone their advocacy skills by making presentations that are videotaped and critiqued. Six additional classrooms accommodate lectures, distance learning, and computer training. Trainees, traveling from throughout the United States to attend courses ranging from two days to two weeks, stay in the center's 264 hotel rooms, study and practice courtroom techniques in video-equipped breakout rooms, take their meals in the double-height south-facing dining room, and relax in the library, lounge, or fitness room.

Sited at the dividing line between the historic core of the 1802 campus, with its "horseshoe" lawn ringed by two- and three-story brick and stucco buildings, and the university's east campus, home to an unfortunately brutal and mismatched collection of post–World War II structures, our design unequivocally rejects the missteps of the university's recent past, distributing the large program in an H-shaped composition of pavilioned wings enclosing garden courtyards. In its massing, detailing, and golden-rose-colored stucco cladding, the center recalls the spare classicism of Robert Mills and Peter Branner, who first shaped the campus.

1. Perspective of south lawn
2. Site plan with ground-floor plan
3. South facade of commons building
4. Residential pavilion

1

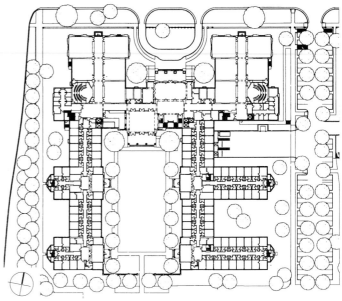

2

0   10   20   40 ft

3

4

Life Dream House

1994

216 Most Americans buy the house they hate the least. In an effort to help improve the quality of builder's houses, *Life* magazine inaugurated its annual "dream house" feature by commissioning from us a design for a small, affordable house. A compact shingled mass relieved by porches, shuttered windows, and dormers, our house was planned to meet a number of different but typical site conditions. In addition, different levels of detailing and finish appropriate to a wide variety of building budgets were possible.

The house proved to be very popular, with *Life* offering its readers the opportunity to purchase working drawings. As a result, many variations have been built across the country without our direct involvement. But one example was constructed under our supervision by a developer, Macauley Homes, in the Legacy Park planned neighborhood in Kennesaw, Georgia, just outside of Atlanta.

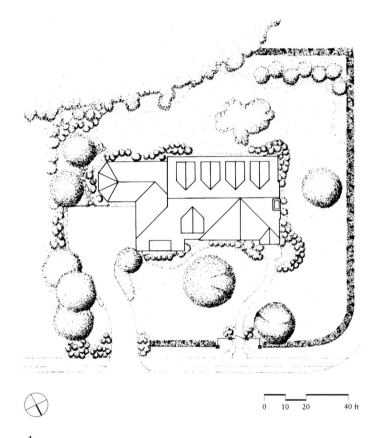

0 10 20 40 ft

1

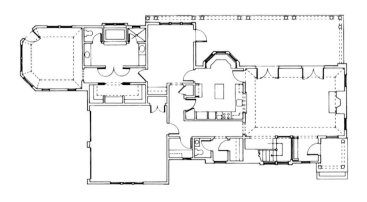

0 5 10 20 ft

2

3

4

5. Porch of Kennesaw model house
6. Great room of Kennesaw model house
7. Porch facade of Wickford Point, Rhode Island, model house
8 (overleaf). Porch facade of Kennesaw model house

6

7

Temple Emanu-el

Closter, New Jersey
1994–

222   With post–World War II suburbanization, many new synagogues were built; few had any architectural distinction, though many had pretensions. Congregation Emanu-el built such a facility in Englewood in 1958–60 and added onto it so much that it had outgrown the site it had occupied since 1928, leading to the decision to relocate to a new, more expansive site in the nearby town of Closter.

Our design arranges spaces for the three characteristic elements of this building type—worship, fellowship, and education—in a U-shaped plan surrounding a meditation garden. Local stone, stucco, and slate roofs are proposed to harmonize with the natural setting, but the composition is strictly disciplined with details that explore traditional Judaic motifs in order to help ground the new worship center in a specific place and culture.

1. Site plan
2. Ground-floor plan
3. View of entrance from southwest
4. View from southeast
5. South elevation

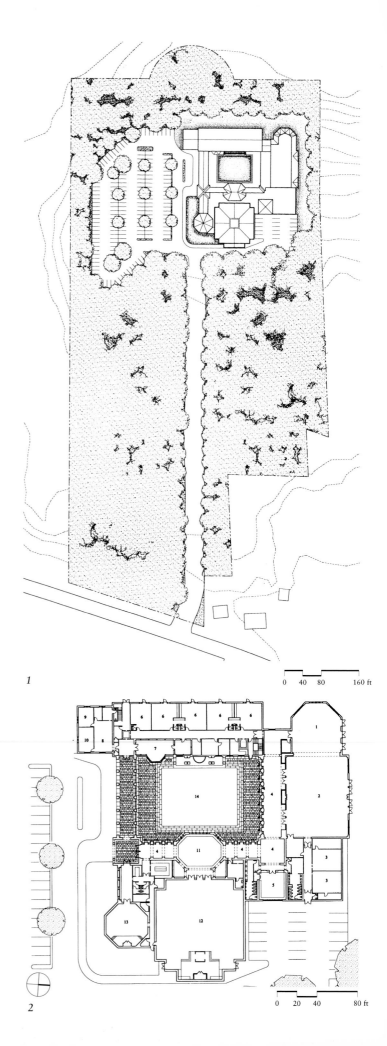

3

4

5

Math/Science Building and Library, Taft School

Watertown, Connecticut
1994

1. Main-level plan
2. Site plan
3. View from southeast
4. View of library facade from south

224 During major building campaigns in the early twentieth century, the Taft School, designed in an almost seamless fashion by Bertram G. Goodhue and James Gamble Rogers, was in effect one building. The composition was unified by a common architectural vocabulary and use of materials designed not to identify specifically the various functions housed within but to celebrate the institution as a whole. With the construction in 1960 and 1968 of the School's Math/Science Building and the Hulbert Taft, Jr., Library, respectively, the school abandoned this tradition for buildings that identified with a single use, jarring the architectural identity. Each of these new buildings was also fundamentally flawed in its siting: the main entrance of the Taft Library turned away from the school's academic core and opened toward what has subsequently become a residential quadrangle; the Math/Science Building both truncated the pond at the heart of the school and blocked the sweeping view from the school's principal buildings across the playing fields and more distant hills to the north.

Our competition design for a new Math/Science Building was intended as the first step in a phased strategy that would allow the school to improve significantly both its math/science and library facilities, reopen views to the north, reorganize and clarify the principal academic quadrangle, and extend and develop the once clear, but now compromised, architectural identity. We also proposed renovations and additions to the library that would help make it part of the larger whole and help clarify and improve the adjacent outdoor open spaces, most notably the principal academic quadrangle. The most significant portion of the site work would accompany the demolition of the existing Math/Science Building, which would open the long-lost vista north from the school's academic quadrangle, allowing the school once again to front on its playing fields instead of backing on them.

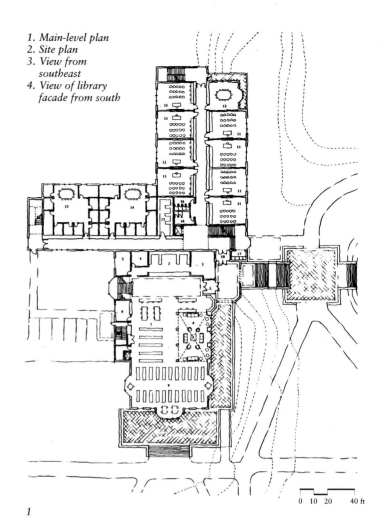

1

0 10 20   40 ft

2

0 50 100   200 ft

225

3

4

Porto Sauipe Marina Village

Bahia, Salvador, Brazil
1994

226   Planned as part of a large-scale equatorial resort community, Marina Village is to function not only as a gateway to the beach for upland residents but also as a destination in its own right, combining the intimacy of a small village and the variety of a much larger town. Not just a street lined with hotels, as is typical of many new Brazilian resorts, Marina Village is planned with an intricate system of public streets, spaces, and buildings in a hierarchy of sizes, shapes, and styles that together create a varied menu of interesting experiences and types of accommodation for the visitor. While most transportation is to be handled by various resort-wide systems, car parking is provided on streets and in small tree-covered lots.

The hotels and *pousadas* (Brazilian bed-and-breakfasts), which make up the majority of the village's building mass are broken down into small structures like those that might be expected in a village, with architectural imagery based on the simple structures typical of small seaside towns. The primary streets are characterized by colorful buildings reminiscent of the Old Town district (the Pelourinho) in nearby Salvador. Even these buildings, as they approach the beach and the golf course, become stylistically less grand and more vernacular.

SITE PLAN
MARINA VILLAGE
PORTO SAUIPE, BRAZIL

0 50 100   200 m

1

2

3

4

Pacific Heights Residence

San Francisco, California
1994–1998

228 The fact that strict zoning and zealously protected view corridors played a dramatic role in shaping our design should not be seen as a negative. On the contrary, we believe that these very constraints have a positive side, fostering an architecture that elsewhere might seem idiosyncratic but here can be justified as site-specific. Looking back to the work of Ernest Coxhead, Bernard Maybeck, and Willis Polk, among other early-twentieth-century architects who helped establish San Francisco's unique tradition of residential architecture, our shingle-clad house confronts the street with a two-and-a-half-story asymmetrical mass culminating in a lantern that bathes a central hall in soft light. At the rear, where the steeply sloping site allows the house to enjoy an additional floor, a symmetrical flat facade is relieved by an overscaled bay window that offers sweeping views across the marina district to San Francisco Bay.

1. *Section facing west*
2. *First-floor plan*
3. *Site plan*
4. *Front facade*
5. *Garden facade*

1

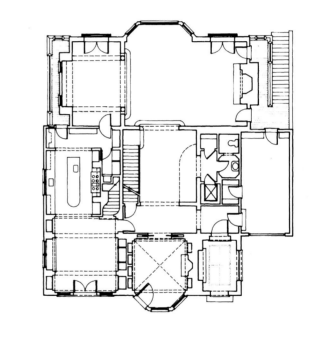

2

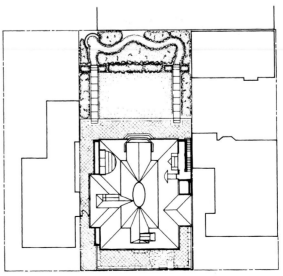

3

4

5

U.S. Courthouse
and IRS Complex

Beckley, West Virginia
1994–1999

230 The three components of the new federal complex—the courthouse, the IRS facility, and the civic lobby—are organized along a pedestrian arcade that in effect extends Main Street into the center of the site. From both the ceremonial Main Street and the more workaday First Avenue site entry points, this arcade leads to the centrally located, top-lit civic lobby that celebrates the public nature of the complex.

The design places court activities at the eastern portion of the site, thereby ensuring a "court" presence on Main Street, where the facade proclaims the dignity of the law. The composition includes various scale-giving elements that complement Beckley's existing civic buildings. The south garden—a landscaped area comprising a fountain, a wide terrace, low plantings, and a ribbon of trees along the arcade—tranforms a nondescript "backyard" area into a parklike public space, adding prestige to the building, enriching the day-to-day downtown journeys of Beckley citizens, and encouraging the positive perception of the federal government in Beckley.

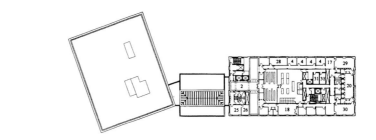

2

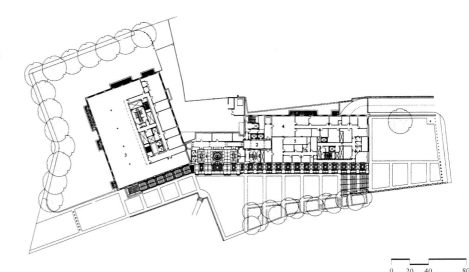

3

1

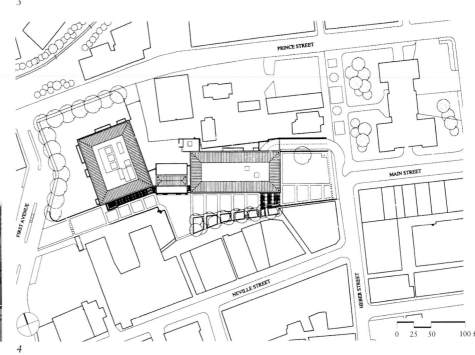

4

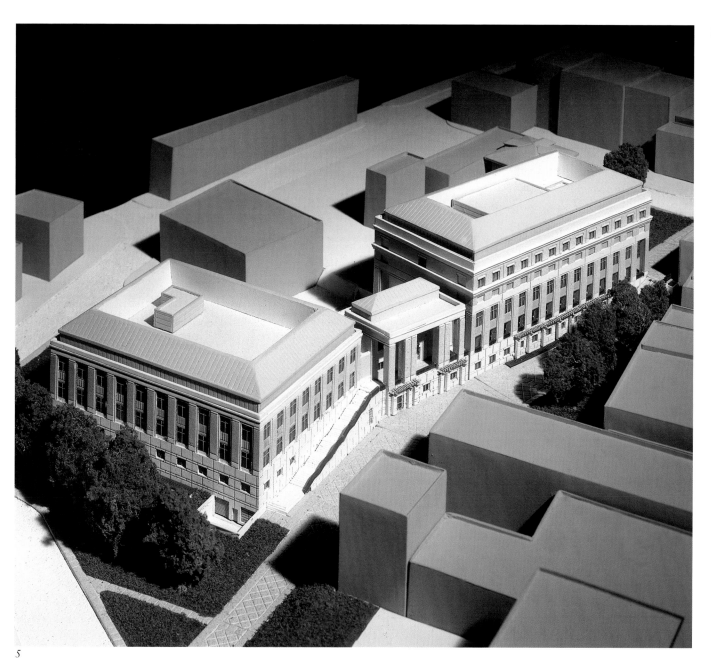

6

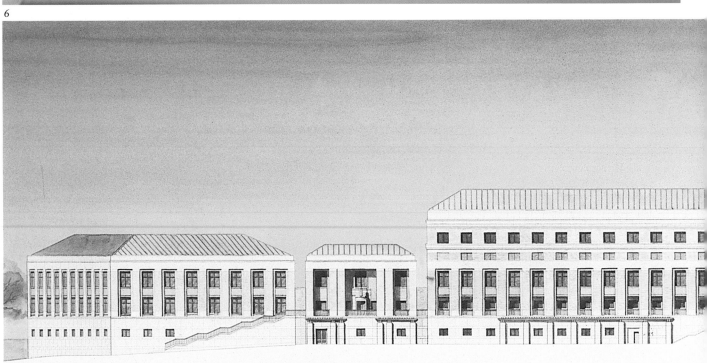

7

8

600 Thirteenth Street, N.W.

Washington, D.C.
1994–1997

1. *East elevation*
2. *Second-floor plan*
3. *Ground-floor plan*
4. *Northwest corner of Thirteenth and F Streets*

234   Covering the full width of the city block between F and G Streets, this eleven-story office building reflects the classicism characteristic of Washington's pre-1950s major institutional and commercial buildings. It refers to the high Roman idiom of the Mall and the simpler, modernizing idiom of the commercial buildings of the 1930s and 1940s. The essentially flat, 260-foot-long facade is articulated with pedimented towerlike pavilions, each supporting terra-cotta-tiled openwork temple fronts that, together with the open-air drums at each end of the roof, introduce a sense of spatial articulation and skyline to what is too often perceived as a city of flattop boxes.

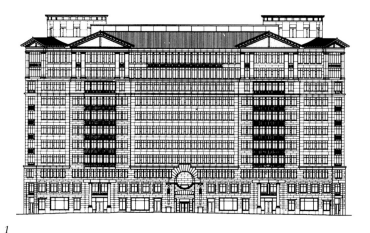

1

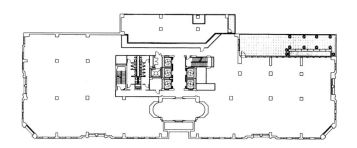

2

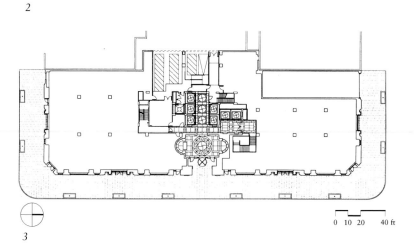

0 10 20   40 ft

3

236

5. *Thirteenth Street retail entrance*
6. *Thirteenth Street office entrance*
7. *Entrance lobby*

5

6

8. *View north along Thirteenth Street*
9. *Office entrance*

9

Residence in Southampton

Southampton, New York
1994–1997

240 Because the site for this house, the last undeveloped part of a subdivided farm, was entirely featureless, the main house, guest house, swimming pool, and tennis court were located so that each provided a focal point to the others, with the large central area left as an open lawn. In the main house, we played formality and informality against each other. Both entry and garden wings of the central block are symmetrical but are flanked by asymmetrical wings to syncopate the overall composition. On the other hand, the guest house is completely casual, with hipped and gabled forms combined to create a compact though cottagelike object. Details of trim, cornices, and windows from the main house are repeated on the guest house to relate the two.

1. West facade of main house
2. East facade of guest house
3. Site plan
4. First-floor plan

1

2

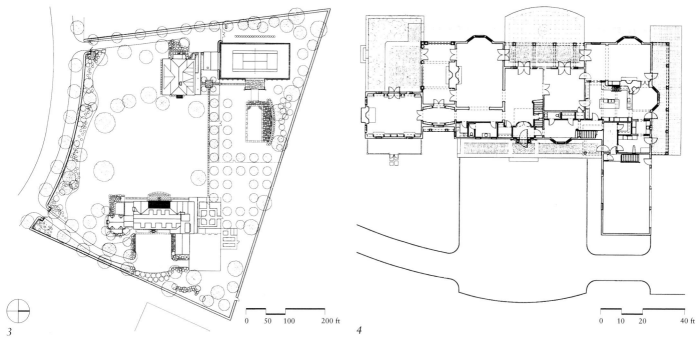

3

4

0   50   100   200 ft

0   10   20   40 ft

Prototypical Stores
for eighteen 77

Short Hills, New Jersey
King of Prussia, Pennsylvania
Woodfield Center, Illinois
1994–1996

242   A prototype for a chain of men's clothing
stores to be built in shopping malls
nationwide, the design of eighteen 77
was part of a year-long effort to assist the
client in defining the new enterprise and
finding a niche for it in a market already
served by clever retailers like the Gap,
Banana Republic, and Polo. To reflect a
marketing strategy that holds that nature,
the machine, and hard work can coexist
in easy harmony, natural materials were
used but not in an overtly handcrafted
way: a precisely machined wood pergola
carried on smoothly finished limestone
piers leads to a vaulted copper canopy
supported by light struts, evoking
nineteenth-century engineering. Inside,
areas containing different types of
merchandise are treated as bays in a
market building, with stone columns
and birch beams carrying a basketweave
of canopylike fabric panels.

1. *Shopfront and entrance, Short Hills*
2. *Short Hills floor plan*
3. *King of Prussia floor plan*
4. *Store interior, Short Hills*

1

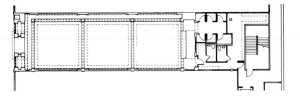

2

3

0   10   20   40 ft

4

Saigon Metropolitan Tower

Ho Chi Minh City (Saigon), Vietnam
1994

244 Despite the clash of scale, skyscrapers need not be alien intruders in established low-lying neighborhoods of traditional architecture. Amid colonial buildings of some distinction and great charm, our proposed tower would have risen in a series of set-back volumes that reduced its apparent size on the skyline. At the base, public arcades, in keeping with the neighborhood pattern, wrapped the building, permitting retail uses while not compromising the overall dignity of the design.

1. Elevation detail at arcade
2. Ground-floor plan
3. Second-floor plan
4. View from Basilica Square

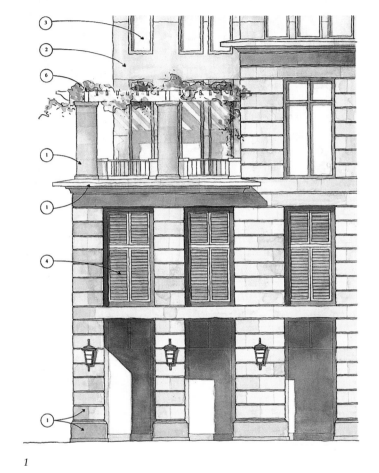

1

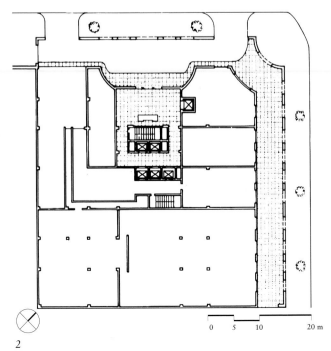

0   5   10   20 m

2

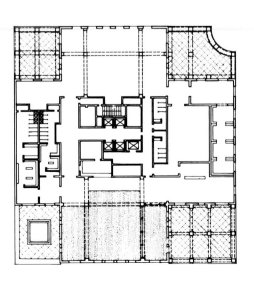

3

Navesink Residence

Middletown, New Jersey
1994–1999

1. First-floor plan
2. Site plan
3. North elevation
4. South elevation
5. View from south
6. View from northwest

246   This house merges the eighteenth-century chateaus found in northwestern Normandy with the more intimately scaled *hôtels particuliers* in and around Versailles. The house is located on a peninsula that projects into the Navesink River. It is specifically sited to take advantage of the dramatic views up- and down-river and to provide ample rolling lawns for recreation. The formal allée and courtyard on the north contrast with the more picturesque landscape on the south.

The austere and classical central portion of the house is organized in a typical French manner with the main entertainment spaces forming an enfilade along the south side. The masses of the family and service wings break down into a picturesque composition. The predominant materials are Texas limestone, stucco, and slate.

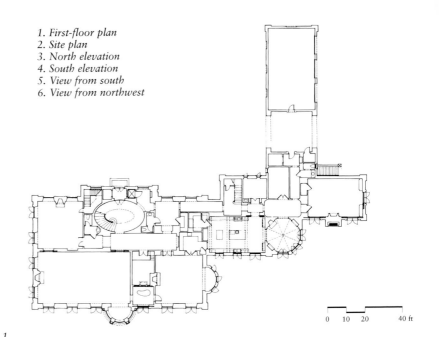

1

0 10 20   40 ft

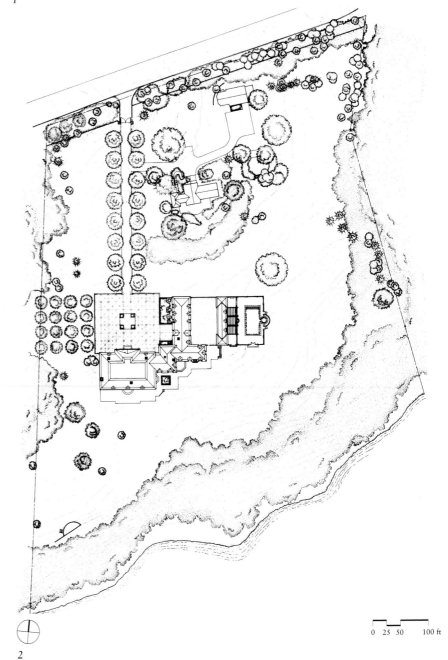

0 25 50   100 ft

2

3

4

5

6

Residence Hall for Columbia University

New York, New York
1996–2000

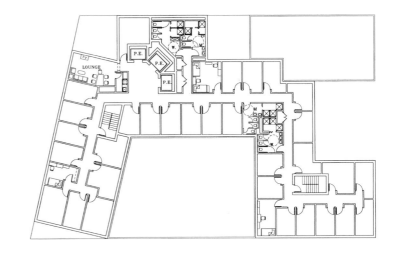

1

248   In 1994 Columbia proposed pulling down Woodbridge Hall and some adjoining townhouses and replacing them with a 427-bed student residence hall as well as facilities for the Korean Church and Institute, which owned and occupied one of the townhouses on the site. We welcomed the opportunity to help create a much-needed facility on a prominent site on Riverside Drive at 115th Street, one that by virtue of its parkfront location would give Columbia a more public face than its inland, introspective McKim, Mead & White campus permitted. But the site proved controversial in the community, which pointed out the historical importance of Woodbridge Hall, the oldest apartment house on Morningside Heights, and decried the loss of the rowhouses and with them mid-block scale. As a result Columbia agreed to relocate the project to another site, at the northeast corner of Broadway and 113th Street, a long-neglected location owned in part by the city, which had acquired it for a branch library.

In early 1996, we were asked to prepare designs for a building on the 113th Street site, incorporating a residence hall, retail space, and the branch library. Our initial design called for a twenty-one-story building that maximized light and views to students' rooms; it was criticized for its height by some community members. Through a series of discussions with well-organized and preservation-minded local residents, the design evolved into a lower, fourteen-story building rising without intermediate setbacks in the manner of the characteristic pre–World War I apartment buildings that line Broadway on Morningside Heights. Our design, C-shaped in plan with a south-facing courtyard, marries the mid-rise scale along Broadway with the lower town-house scale along 113th Street and incorporates significant portions of an early Morningside Heights townhouse designed in 1903 by the architect George Keister.

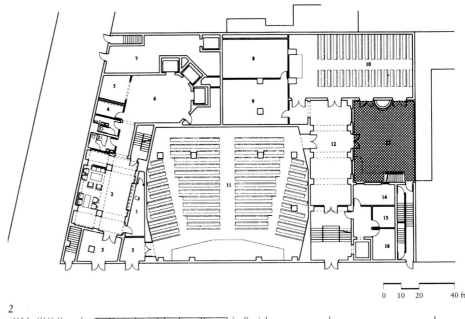

2

0 10 20   40 ft

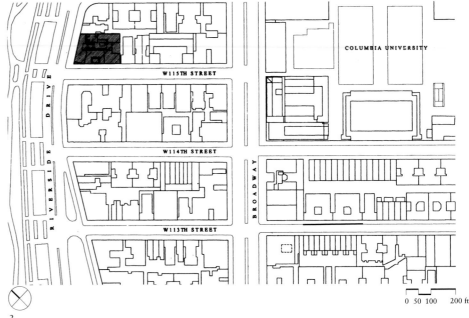

3

0 50 100   200 ft

1. *Residence hall floor plan,*
   floors three through nine
   (115th Street and Riverside Drive site)
2. *Ground-floor plan*
   (115th Street and Riverside Drive site)
3. *Site plan*
   (115th Street and Riverside Drive site)
4. *View from west across Riverside Drive*
   (115th Street and Riverside Drive site)
5. *View from northwest*
   (115th Street and Riverside Drive site)

4

5

6. *View from southwest (twenty-one-story tower at 113th Street and Broadway site)*
7. *113th Street and Broadway site*
8. *Site plan (113th Street and Broadway site)*
9. *View from southwest (113th Street and Broadway site)*

250

6

7

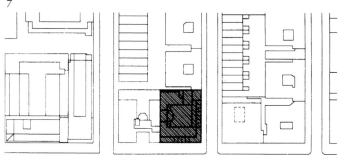

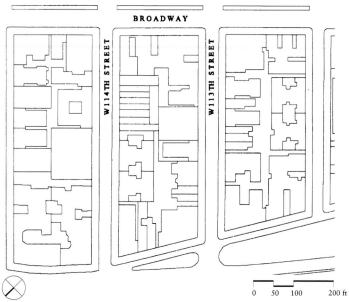

BROADWAY

W 114TH STREET

W 113TH STREET

0   50   100   200 ft

8

10

11

10. South elevation along 113th Street
    (113th Street and Broadway site)
11. West elevation along Broadway
    (113th Street and Broadway site)
12. Ground-floor plan
    (113th Street and Broadway site)
13. Second-floor plan
    (113th Street and Broadway site)
14. Typical floor plan
    (113th Street and Broadway site)

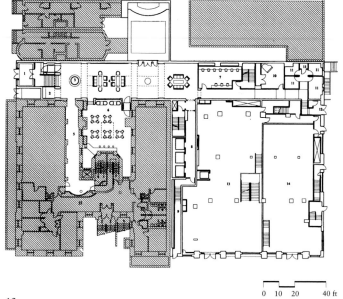

0 10 20   40 ft

12

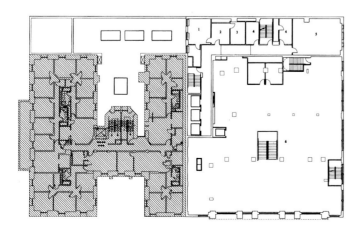

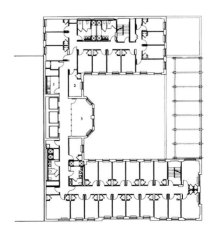

13

14

Residence and Guest House at Katama

Martha's Vineyard, Massachusetts
1995–1997

254 Sited on Katama Bay and enjoying views
of Chappaquiddick Island and the
Atlantic Ocean, the main house and nearby guest house are in keeping with the
severe height restrictions imposed on new
construction in the area. The design
combines elements of vernacular
New England architecture with an overall
massing and character representative of
the Shingle style. The loosely composed
mass of the main house is sheltered under
a gambrel roof that flares widely at the
eaves to create deep covered porches that
extend into a gazebo and screened-porch
pavilion facing the water. Within, the
planning is kept open and informal,
but the detailing is somewhat grander.
The more modest, gambrel-roofed guest
house, sited so that it enjoys a view of
the bay across a sweeping lawn, reiterates
the detailing and casual character of
the main house.

1. *Second-floor plan*
2. *First-floor plan*
3. *Site plan*
4. *Entry facade of main house*
5. *Guest house*

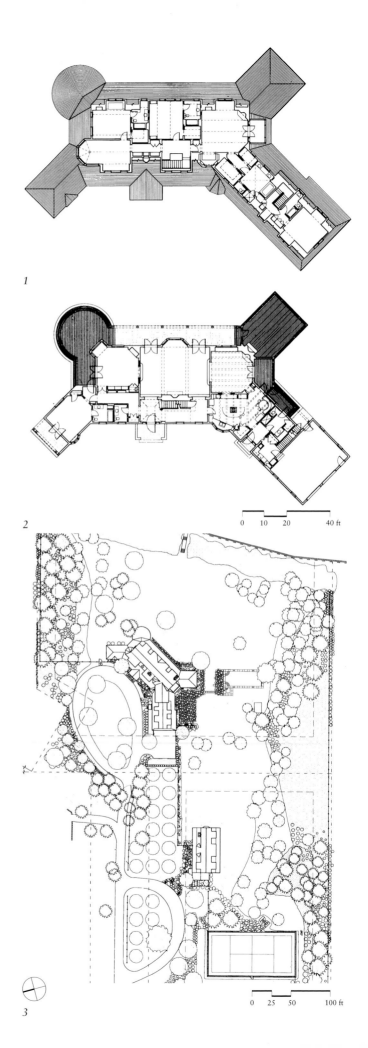

1

2

0 10 20 40 ft

0 25 50 100 ft

3

4

5

6. *Dining room*
7. *Master bedroom*
8. *Living room*

6

7

9. *View from south*
10. *Screened porch*
11. *View from dock*

10

11

U.S. Department of State Office Building Chancery

Berlin, Germany
1995

1. Site plan
2. Aerial perspective view
3. Model photo from Behrenstrasse

260 Virtually unknown as a building type until comparatively recently, the embassy is one of the great challenges of modern practice, incorporating efficient, highly secure office space in a building representative of a nation's highest ideals. In the case of Berlin, the problem was even more complex: the new building needed to be a diplomatic gesture honoring not only our country but also the architecture of a historically charged setting. Our design was prepared as part of an extremely detailed competition organized by the State Department. We did not win, in part because it was felt that our strategy of inserting an exceptional element, the glass-roofed atrium, within a classical frame, was unresolved. From our perspective, the tension between the two modes of composition not only enriched the experience of the building but also exemplified in a positive manner the condition imposed by Berlin authorities to honor the city's traditional plan yet foster architectural experimentation.

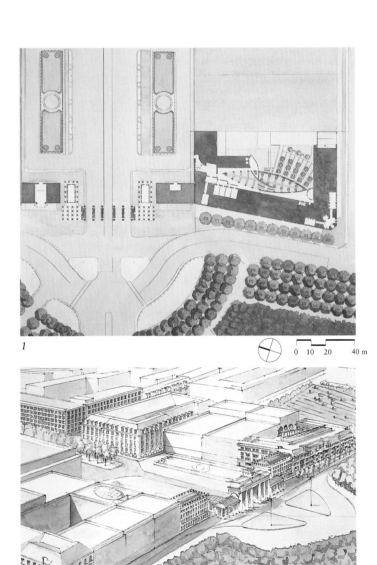

1

0 10 20   40 m

2

4

4. *Model photo from Ebertstrasse looking*
   toward Brandenburg Gate
5. *Model photo from Pariser Platz*

263

5

Newport Bay Club Convention Center

Paris Disneyland, France
1995–1997

264 To help support the year-round business viability of Paris Disneyland, a 110,000-square-foot convention center has been added to the Newport Bay Club, an 1,100-room hotel we built in 1992; the new facility carries forward the language of the hotel. The convention center can be entered through a new entrance leading to a forty-foot-high barrel-vaulted lobby open to a cupola that allows natural light to stream down from above. Beyond the lobby, the main ballroom, capable of seating 1,500 people, contains a proscenium stage with a fly loft and retractable orchestra pit. Despite the large size and fundamental inward orientation, the plan is organized and the building is massed to suggest a village of forms rather than a monolith.

1. *Cupola at main entrance*
2. *Location plan*
3. *View from northeast*
4. *View from northwest*

1

HOTEL CHEYENNE

HOTEL SANTE FE

HOTEL NEW YORK

To Park

SEQUOIA LODGE

FESTIVAL
DISNEY

NEWPORT BAY CLUB

NEWPORT BAY CLUB
CONVENTION CENTER

0   150   300   600 m

2

3, 4

266

5

6

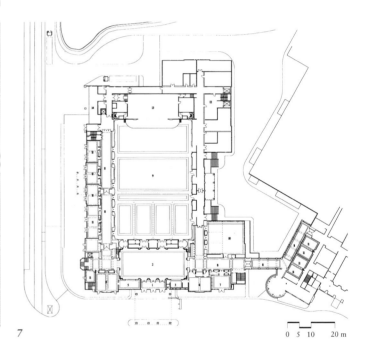

7

0 5 10   20 m

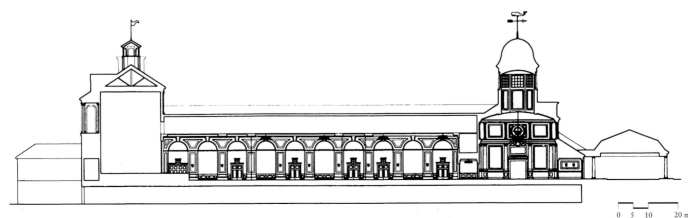

8

0 5 10   20 m

Master Plan and Addition to Knott Science Center, College of Notre Dame of Maryland

Baltimore, Maryland
1995–

1. West elevation, with addition
   to Knott Science Center at left
2. Second-floor plan
3. Ground-floor plan
4. Campus master plan
5. Aerial view of campus

270

The College of Notre Dame of Maryland is the oldest Catholic women's college in North America. Founded in 1873, its buildings crown a hill on a spacious suburban site. Challenged by the competition for students with small coeducational institutions, and by the need to strengthen its programs, especially in the sciences, the college commissioned a master plan to help guide physical growth in its second century. The master plan reorganizes roads and parking to create a formal college walk and to make room for expanded sports fields as well as a number of new buildings and additions. The first of these will be the addition to the Knott Science Center, where a new forty-thousand-square-foot wing will provide state-of-the-art laboratories, support space, classrooms, and offices, as well as a dignified entrance to what was, at best, a workhorse building from the 1950s. Stylistically, the new wing refers to the Gothic of Gibbons Hall (1873), the college's first, and still most important, building.

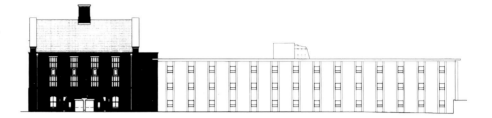

1

2

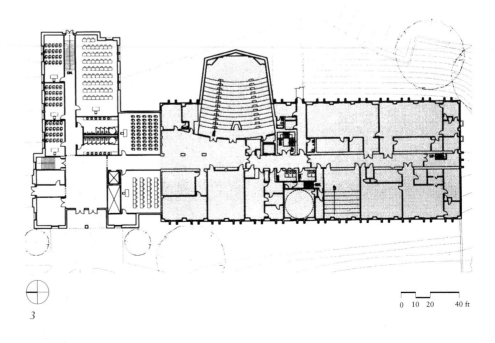

0 10 20   40 ft

3

4

5

Bangor Public Library

Bangor, Maine
1995–1998

272   Bangor's grand, Beaux-Arts classical library, designed in 1914 by the Boston firm of Peabody & Stearns, is a much-beloved and widely patronized institution. Though not without inherent interest, our buff-brick and cast-stone addition defers to the original building, which we have restored, providing new reading and meeting rooms, and at the same time doubling the amount of book space while for the first time creating stacks for public use. At the base of the hingelike tower marking the point of transition between the old and new buildings, a new garden entry provides direct access for disabled people.

1. *View across Harlow Street from south*
2. *Site plan*
3. *View from southwest*

1

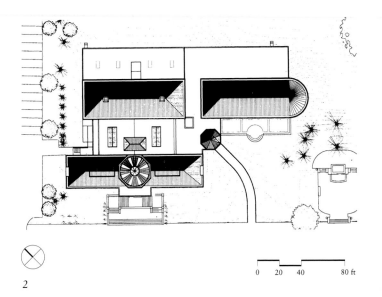

2

0   20   40   80 ft

3

4. Main lobby
5. Main reading room
6. Ground-floor plan
7. Periodicals reading room
8 (overleaf). Periodicals reading room
   and main reading room

4

5

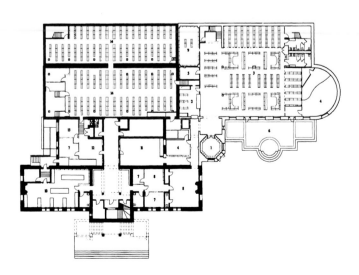

0 10 20   40 ft

6

U.S. Courthouse Annex

Savannah, Georgia
1995–

Understandably the Savannah community was very concerned about how the new 165,000-square-foot annex to the U.S. Post Office and Courthouse (William Aiken, 1896; James A. Wetmore, 1931) would fit in with the city's historic architecture and plan, which encompassed an intricate grid of squares, streets, and lanes laid out by James Oglethorpe in 1733. In an unusual departure from precedent, we were hired by the General Services Administration before a site was chosen and asked to lead the site selection process. Our recommendation, which was adopted, called for demolishing two very unpopular 1980s federal buildings built on narrow so-called trust lots immediately to the west of the existing courthouse and closing the intervening street to create a site large enough to house a new court building that would complement the height and character of the existing courthouse.

Our annex is a quiet interpretation of Aiken's elaborately detailed building and Wetmore's complementary addition. The annex will use many of the original building's materials: Cherokee white Georgia marble from the same quarry and terra-cotta roofing tiles. Its details,

though related to the original Italian Renaissance Revival building, are more abstract, so that traditional and familiar features are restated in relation to contemporary conditions.

Following the construction of the annex, the existing courthouse will be renovated, and at that time the 1931 entrance from Wright Square will be reinstated as the principal entrance to the court complex. Nonetheless, the annex will enjoy an important presence on Telfair Square, where a triple-arched loggia will form an equally important entrance. To ensure that the buildings will not only look but also function as a unit, the annex will be connected to the existing courthouse by three separate tunnels under Whitaker Street, providing secure access for the public, judges, and prisoners. The public tunnel will lead to a glass-roofed courtyard that may be used for community gatherings. From the courtyard, a grand staircase will lead through an enfilade of public lobbies and onto a security lobby and secondary entrance facing Telfair Square, or up to a second skylit courtyard created out of the service area of the post office that formerly occupied the ground floor of the historic courthouse.

2

1

1. *Existing U.S. Post Office and Courthouse*
2. *Facade detail*
3. *Plan showing annex at left and existing courthouse at right*
4. *View from Telfair Square*
5. *Barnard Street elevation*

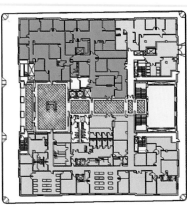

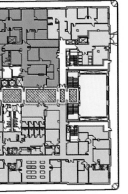

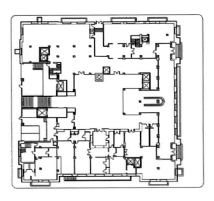

3

0 5 10   20 m

4

5

South Campus Housing, West Quadrangle, University of South Carolina

Columbia, South Carolina
1995–1997

1. Second-floor plan
2. Campus plan
3. East courtyard
4. West courtyard

280   A deliberate effort to recapture the university's traditional architectural character while accommodating current trends in student life, the four-hundred-student facility is located in an area bereft of architectural distinction at the fringes of South Carolina's sprawling campus. To attract independent-minded upper-year students who normally flee conventional dormitories for off-campus apartments, the new building is a hybrid, providing four-bedroom apartments comparable to those typically found off-campus in subdivided houses, but adding the benefit of a shared community by arranging them along a corridor as in a dormitory or a large-scale apartment house. A commons area housing student lounges, meeting rooms, and administrative offices is located at the nexus of circulation between our two courtyards and a future residential development to the east, further enhancing the social dimension.

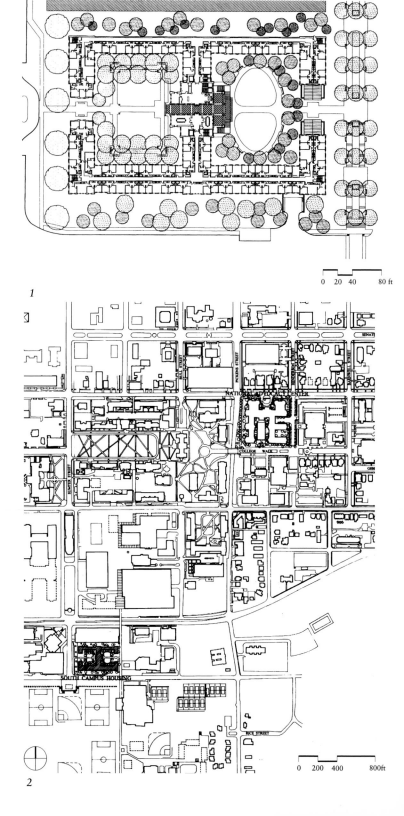

0   20   40   80 ft

1

0   200   400   800ft

2

3

4

5. *South facade*
6. *Gatehouse*
7. *Open passageway*
8. *South facade*

282

5

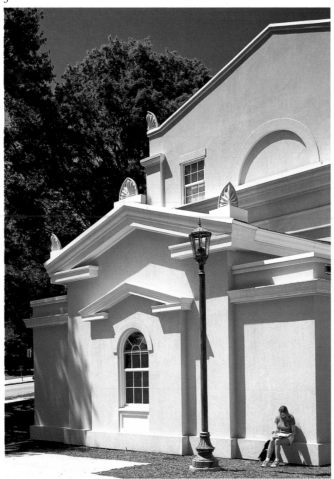

6

7

284

9. *Lounge*
10. *Lounge detail*
11. *Meeting room*
12. *Stair hall*

9

10

11

Spring Valley Residence

Washington, D.C.
1995–

286 Our clients, who currently lease a Federal-style house by John Russell Pope, very much want a house of similar character but with more space. They were able to obtain a large site in the northwest corner of Washington, for which we designed this cubic, geometrically disciplined homage to Pope; it will be realized in a mix of five different hues of red brick. Though the setting is distinctly suburban, we have given the house a more urban character by siting it at the street line setback; the main block of the house, family wing, and service wing are arranged to form a garden courtyard sheltered from the street by high walls.

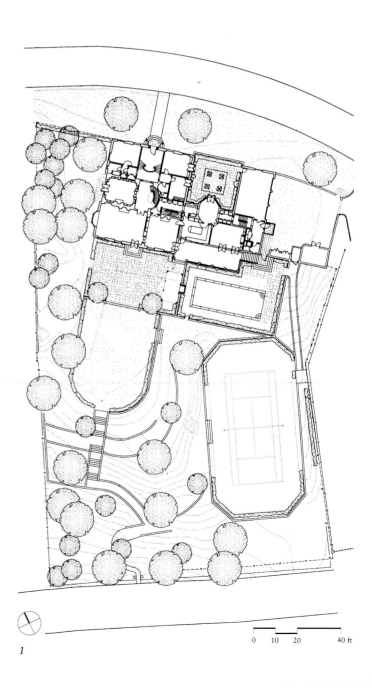

0   10   20   40 ft

1

2

3

Union Square South

New York, New York
1995

288 The south side of Union Square is one of
the most visible locations in Manhattan,
commanding long vistas up and down
Park Avenue and Broadway. Our competition proposal for a 380,000-square-foot
building at the intersection of Fourteenth
Street and Park Avenue South, facing
Union Square, consists of an eighteen-
story apartment tower on a five-story
retail base. The stone-clad base was to
follow the property line, maintaining the
street edge, while the apartment tower
above, set back from the property line
to create a strong south terminus for
the Park Avenue view corridor, was
to be sheathed in brick with metal
pilasters and projecting slabs to recall
the column and cornice articulation
of prewar architecture, but in a more
severely modern way.

1. *View down Park Avenue*
2. *Typical floor plan*
3. *Ground-floor plan*
4. *View from Union Square*

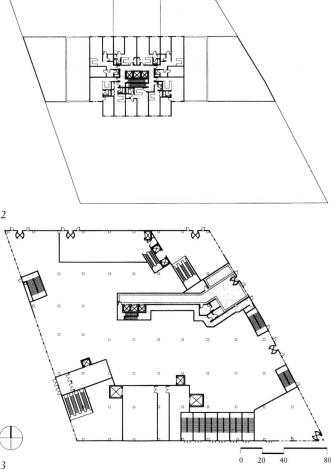

1

2

3

0   20   40   80 ft

4

Yawkey Park

Boston, Massachusetts
1995

290   Working as part of a large team, we developed a conceptual design for a forty-six-thousand-seat baseball park for the Boston Red Sox on a thirteen-acre site fronting on Fort Point Channel in central Boston. The site, constrained by robust, nineteenth-century warehouses on two sides and by the channel on a third side, resulted in an asymmetrical playing field incorporating many of the idiosyncrasies that give Fenway Park, the existing Red Sox ballpark, its unique character. The Green Monster, a time-honored fixture at Fenway, is replicated and supplemented by the waterway, well within reach of a left-field home-run fly ball. The sequence of public spaces surrounding the park is carefully choreographed to add to and take advantage of before- and after-game pedestrian activity. A pedestrian "street" is squeezed between the proposed ballpark and an adjacent loft building housing restaurants and shops; it is spanned by bridges connecting the ballpark at its upper level to office space and club facilities. Between the ballpark and Fort Point Channel, a pedestrian boardwalk offers waterfront dining and strolling and space for ferry docking and marina tailgating. The north-northwest orientation of the park focuses views beyond the playing field to the adjacent Boston skyline.

1. *View across Fort Point Channel*
2. *Aerial view*
3. *Pedestrian street along east side of ballpark*
4. *Pedestrian bridge connecting ballpark to member clubhouse*

1

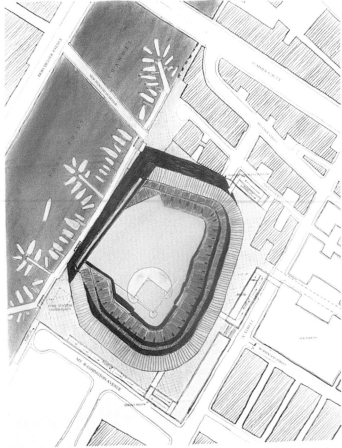

2

3

4

Tribeca Park

Battery Park City,
New York, New York
1995–1999

292   In designing this 396-unit black-granite-and-limestone-trimmed red-brick apartment house, one of the first three to be located at the northern end of Battery Park City in Manhattan, we have departed from the genteel, Riverside Drive–inspired aesthetic previously pursued elsewhere in the development. We selected a tougher, bolder vocabulary of hard edges, bold bracketed overhangs, and colossally scaled columnar elements that we believe will visually unite the building with the nearby Tribeca warehouse district. Construction began in February 1998.

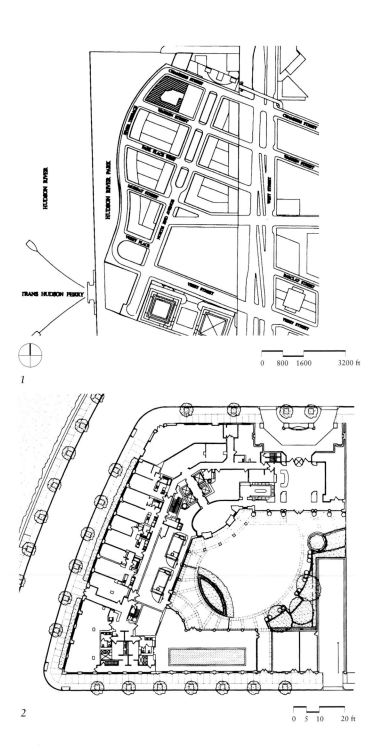

1

0   800 1600   3200 ft

2

0 5 10   20 ft

4

294

5

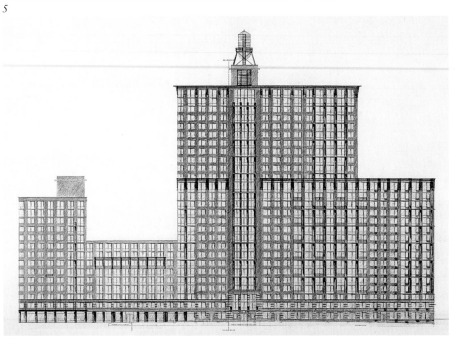

6

Edison Field

Anaheim, California
1995–1998

1. Existing stadium
2. Main entrance plaza at Homeplate Building
3. Field-level plan
4. Aerial view

296 This renovation, which transformed a rather brutish stadium built in 1966 for baseball but renovated in 1980 to accommodate football into a "ballpark," was accomplished in two major construction campaigns so that no games were missed. We removed the stands installed for football and reconfigured the seating so that forty-five thousand fans of the Anaheim Angels baseball team are now accommodated in stands and club suites, including ten suites behind home plate at the dugout level.

Ringing the stands, a new parklike apron containing picnic and refreshment areas for pre- and postgame activities forms a buffer to the surrounding parking. Suddenly, what had been a stadium in the middle of a parking lot has become a true ballpark. A new plaza, in the form of a baseball diamond, which is flanked by shaded shelters in the form of super-scaled baseball caps, leads to a boldly reconfigured entrance, dramatizing arrival and injecting a sense of fun and occasion into what had hitherto been a ho-hum setting for the national pastime.

2

1

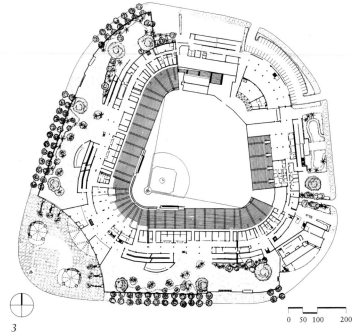

3

0   50 100   200 ft

5

6

7

5. *Competition perspective showing view of outfield from I-55*
6. *Competition view of club level and restaurant and apron area*
7. *Competition perspective showing view from stadium club*
8. *Entrance*

Miller Field

Milwaukee, Wisconsin
1995

1. Concourse-level plan
2. Location plan
3. Exterior view with roof closed
4. Interior view with roof closed

300   Our competition proposal for the new forty-five-thousand-seat Miller Field for the Milwaukee Brewers was sited in a location where its construction would not interrupt operation of the existing ballpark. The ballpark was intended as the focal point of broad, radial walkways leading up from the parking lots, where fans traditionally gather before games for tailgate parties. While the owners were convinced that the sometimes inhospitable Wisconsin weather required a retractable roof, our design attempted to minimize this feature in order to capture as much as possible of the character of traditional ballparks. Designed to be opened or closed in seven minutes, midgame if necessary, the roof consists of six gently arching and nested trusses that part over center field and roll on curving tracks to resting places over the side-field concourses. Both translucent fabric and opaque metal-panel roof membranes were studied. The exposed steel trusswork and supporting structure visually connect to the early-twentieth-century mill buildings that face the ballpark across the river, while the limestone-trimmed, buff-brick arches and clay-tile roof of the concourse facades look to the Midwest modernism of Louis Sullivan and the Prairie school.

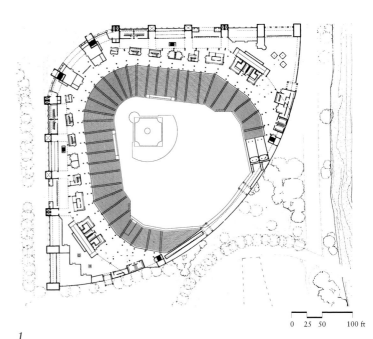

0 25 50   100 ft

1

2

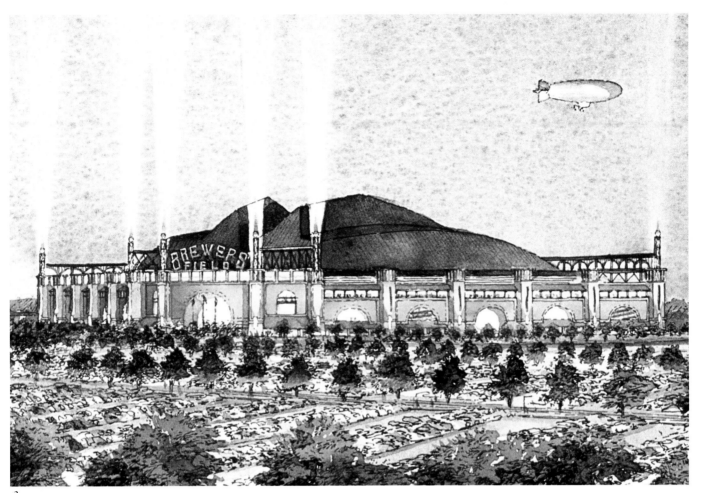

3

4

Residence on Kiawah Island

South Carolina
1995–

302 Facing south toward the Atlantic Ocean across a broad beach, this house is constrained by coastal flood regulations that require it to be set one-half story above natural grade. To reduce the apparent mass, the roof of the two-and-a-half-story central volume steps down in wings to either side; gambrels over most of the house bring the eave down below the second-floor plate. The long, low, and slightly flared roof is punctuated to either side by shed dormers and, at the center, by a gambrel surmounted in turn by a third-story lantern. Gentle angles in the plan allow for a variety of orientations and views along the beach, and for the tentative formation of an entrance forecourt at the north.

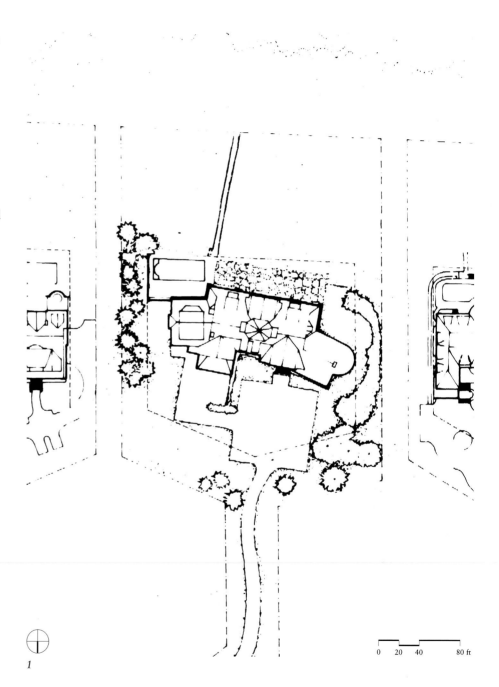

1

0   20   40   80 ft

2

3

4

0 5 10 20 ft

Disney Ambassador Hotel

Urayasu-shi, Chiba-ken, Japan
1996–

304   This five-hundred-room hotel—designed for the Oriental Land Company as the first Disney-branded hotel in Japan—is part of a new development at the gateway to the resort emerging around Tokyo Disneyland and the announced Tokyo DisneySea theme park. It is adjacent to the Maihama train station, the principal arrival point for visitors to the resort. The art moderne–inspired design looks back to an architecture that represented the promise, magic, and glamour of a time when travel and movies were a romantic escape.

1. *View of pool court*
2. *Site plan*
3. *Ground-floor plan*
4. *West elevation*
5. *South elevation*

1

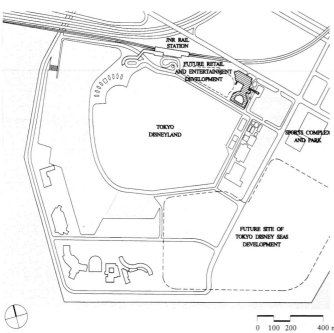

2

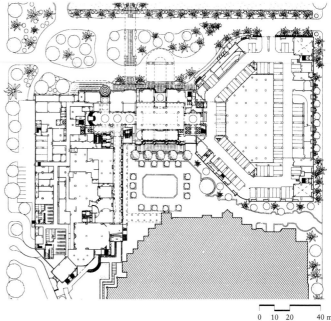

3

4

5

House at the Point

Santa Lucia Preserve,
Monterey County, California
1996

1. Northwest elevation
2. Southeast elevation
3. Ground-floor plan
4. View from southeast
5. Entry court

306 In order to demonstrate a set of guide-lines developed by another firm for this environmentally sensitive residential enclave, we were asked to prepare a design for a house using, as a program, the "dream list" of a potential house-owner who collects antique cars. For the dramatic site on the prow of a hill with views of Potrero Valley to the southeast, we proposed a stucco and tile-roofed house continuing the tradition of Spanish-colonial architecture that has played such an important role in shaping the character of the Monterey region.

Approached from above through a grove of nut trees, the house, massed around a circular entry court, follows the slope so that principal living areas can be situated along the downhill side to take full advantage of light and views. While the courtyard provides a strong statement of arrival, on the downhill side the casual, asymmetrical composition of projecting pavilions and roofed arcades suggests a village or a building that has been modified and added to over time.

1

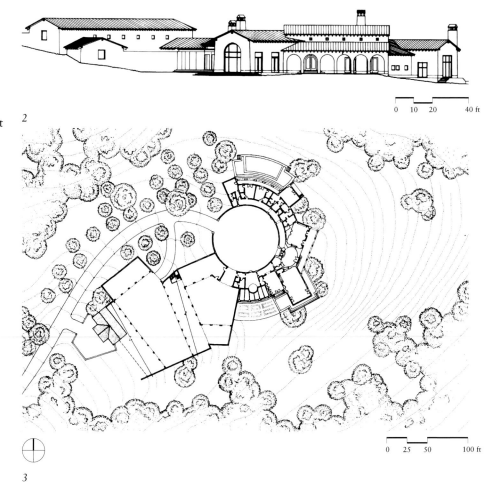

2

0 10 20   40 ft

3

0   25   50   100 ft

4

5

National Storytelling Center

Jonesborough, Tennessee
1996–

308   Each fall, the National Storytelling Association, an organization dedicated to the preservation and promulgation of the rich tradition of oral storytelling, attracts thousands of visitors to its Storytelling Festival in Jonesborough for three days of events held in temporary, circus-style tents scattered around the small, historic city. In an effort to expand the association's operations to year-round programming, the Storytelling Center—complementing the 1780s Chester Inn, newly restored for use as association offices, the post office building, to be restored for research and library functions, and a park—will function as an interactive visitor center. In keeping with Jonesborough's small-town scale, our building is broken into components that negotiate a difficult, steep site. Inside, a variety of spaces are organized around a top-lit, three-story tower.

1. Main Street perspective
2. Site plan
3. Ground-level plan

1

2

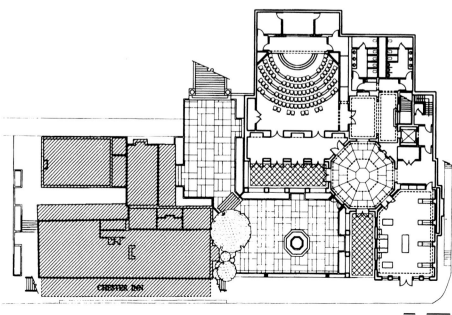

CHESTER INN

0 5 10   20 ft

Mulholland House

Los Angeles, California
1996

310   Dramatically sited high above
Los Angeles, this house, with massing
and architectural vocabulary inspired by
architects who helped shape California
building tradition earlier in the century,
such as Wallace Neff, and by Italian
mountain villas, such as Cuzzano, is
oriented to capture views northeast
across the San Fernando Valley to the
San Gabriels, and southwest across the
Santa Monica Mountains to the Pacific
Ocean. A progression of galleries and
enfilades provides the connective tissue
among the principal rooms of the first
floor; outside, a gently curved loggia
defines a garden room centered
about the swimming pool.

1

2

0   20   40   80 ft

3

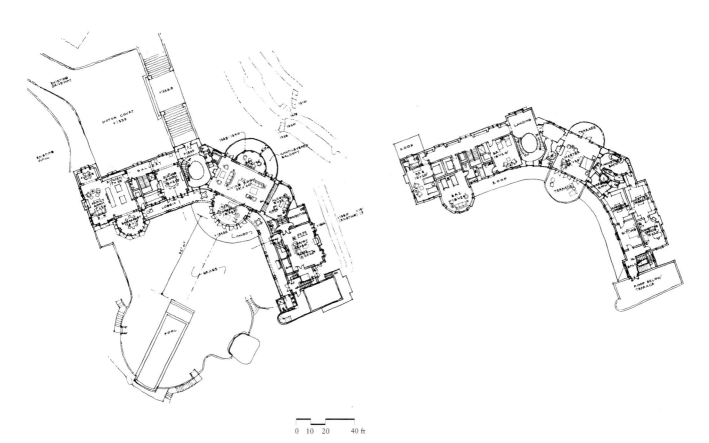

0   10   20   40 ft

4   5

Wellesley Office Park

Wellesley, Massachusetts
1996

Produced as part of a developer's competitive proposal to build 290,000 square feet of multitenant commercial office space on a sixteen-acre former highway maintenance depot at the prime and highly visible intersection of Routes 9 and 128 in the Boston suburb of Wellesley, our design for three brick and limestone buildings of four stories each would frame a south-facing garden courtyard.

2

1

1. *Site plan*
2. *View from south*
3. *View of courtyard*

3

Residence

Greenwich, Connecticut
1994

314   Intended for a large property fronting a small pond, this design, like the many stone "manors" built in Greenwich during the 1920s, draws on Cotswold sources for its character and detail. The use of a red-tile roof, a mix of brick and stone detail, and the softening of the mass by bringing the roof down to the first-floor eaves give the house a more informal character than many of its 1920s antecedents, while the carefully orchestrated exterior spaces—entry court, lakeside terraces, and pool area—are in some ways more distinctly architectural.

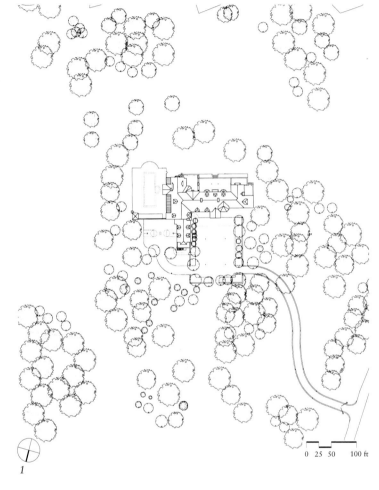

0 25 50   100 ft

1

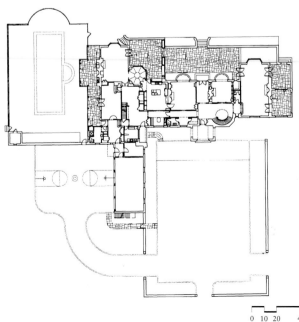

0 10 20   40 ft

2

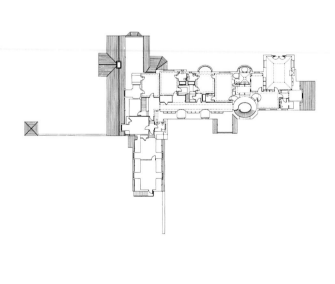

3

4

5

6

Residence

Denver, Colorado
1996–

316 Organized around a series of courtyards and formally defined gardens, this will be one of our most rigorously composed and detailed classical houses. A square motor court marks the beginning of an axial sequence that leads past an elliptical entry hall and stair hall to an enfilade of rooms facing a broad terrace and precisely defined lawn. A strong cross-axis leading from the stair hall through a south-facing courtyard terminates in a rose garden. A wing extending to the north contains athletic facilities, including an indoor pool. While the buff-colored limestone elevations are more French than English, the interior design is Adamesque, with highly keyed colors and dramatic decorative details.

1

2

1. East elevation
2. South elevation
3. Site plan
4. First-floor plan
5. South-north section
6. West-east section

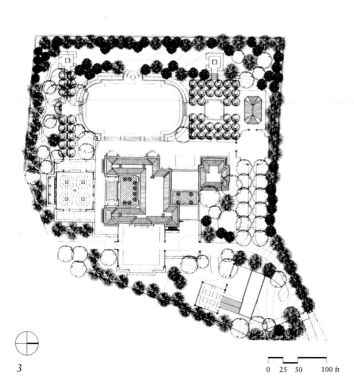

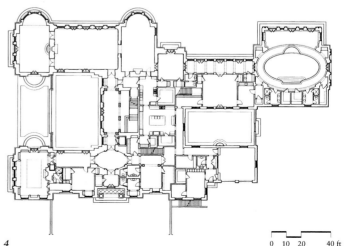

3

0 25 50   100 ft

4

0 10 20   40 ft

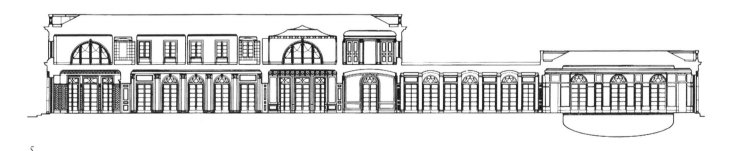

5

6

Federal Reserve Bank of Atlanta Headquarters

Atlanta, Georgia
1996–2001

318   The new Federal Reserve Bank of Atlanta, housing the Sixth Federal Reserve District Headquarters and the Atlanta branch, will occupy a key midtown site on the west side of Peachtree Street between Tenth and Eleventh Streets. The new 750,000-square-foot facility combines a ten-story office tower with a low base housing a conference center as well as facilities for processing checks and cash. The mission of this project is to create a facility that will satisfy the bank's functional requirements, make a positive contribution to the city of Atlanta, and present an image of stability consistent with the bank's role as a model public institution.

Building upon the Sixth Federal Reserve District's own architectural history, and drawing inspiration from Paul Cret's Federal Reserve headquarters in Washington, our design is classical, but in a modern way, with every effort made in the handling of the window wall to set it apart from typical office buildings without sacrificing internal space-planning flexibility. The main entrance is off Peachtree Street, where many visitors arrive, especially tourists and school-children who visit the money museum and tour the facility; to accommodate staff and many visitors who arrive by car, a significant secondary lobby on the third floor serves the parking garage at the building's west end.

1. *View of Tenth Street and Peachtree Street corner from southeast*
2. *First-floor plan*
3. *Site/third-floor plan*
4. *Typical tower-floor plan*

1

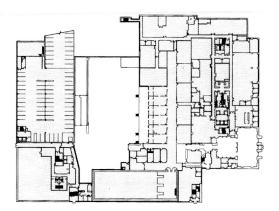

2

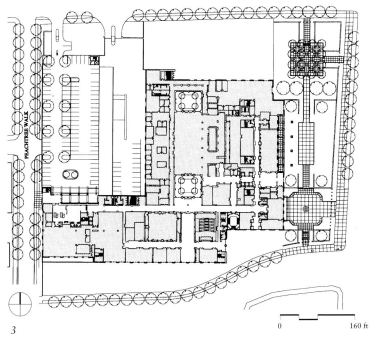

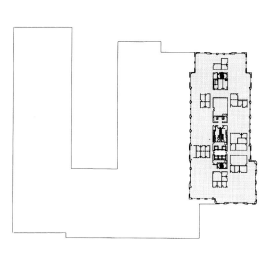

3

0   160 ft   4

Heavenly View Ranch

Old Snowmass, Colorado
1996–1998

At an elevation of 8,700 feet in the Colorado Rockies, this house enjoys the highest, and perhaps the most remote, site we've encountered to date. The house was conceived as a lodge, both in function and design, that would house three generations of a closely knit family for whom we had built a house in Pottersville, New Jersey, ten years before.

We were inspired by the great National Park lodges of the West, which employed a rustic vocabulary of logs, timbers, and rough-hewn stone to provide comfortable and sometimes luxurious accommodations for tourists from the East. At the center of our plan, a spacious, vaulted living room under a spreading gable roof is framed in logs and timber trusses. To one side, the family room is in a tower with vertical proportions that form an architectural counterpoint to the broad expanse of the living room. Lower, shed-roofed wings containing the master suite, kitchen, and service areas connect the primary volumes. Set below the main level and into the side of the ridge are guest suites and an exercise room.

1. Site plan
2. View of living room
3. View of family room
4. Entry facade
5. South facade
6. North elevation

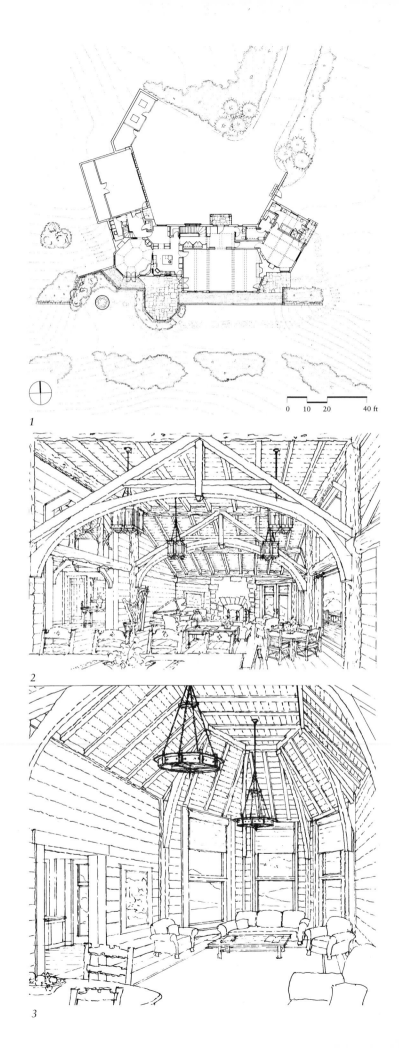

1

0   10   20   40 ft

2

3

4

5

6

Diagonal Mar Entertainment and Retail Center

Barcelona, Spain
1996–

322 Located on the site of an abandoned locomotive factory, now the largest undeveloped site on Barcelona's Mediterranean waterfront, Diagonal Mar combines an urban entertainment and retail center with medium-rise and high-rise residential, hotel, and office development and a thirty-four-acre public park. The development occupies a critical site in the pattern of Barcelona's urban development, at the eastern edge of the city's nineteenth-century Eixample street grid pattern, established by Ildefons

1. *Entertainment-level plan*
2. *Retail center top-floor*
3. *Site plan*
4. *View of retail center from southeast*
5. *Carrer Taulat elevation*
6. *Avinguda Diagonal elevation*
7. *Carrer Josep Pla elevation*

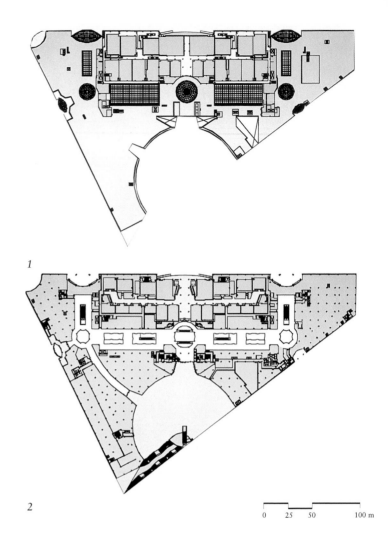

1

2

0   25   50   100 m

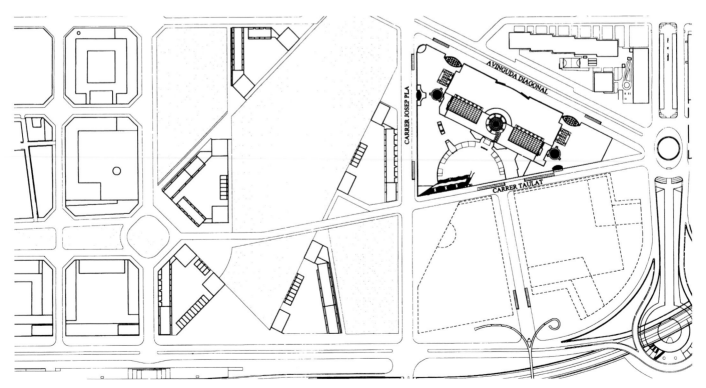

3

0   25   50   100 m

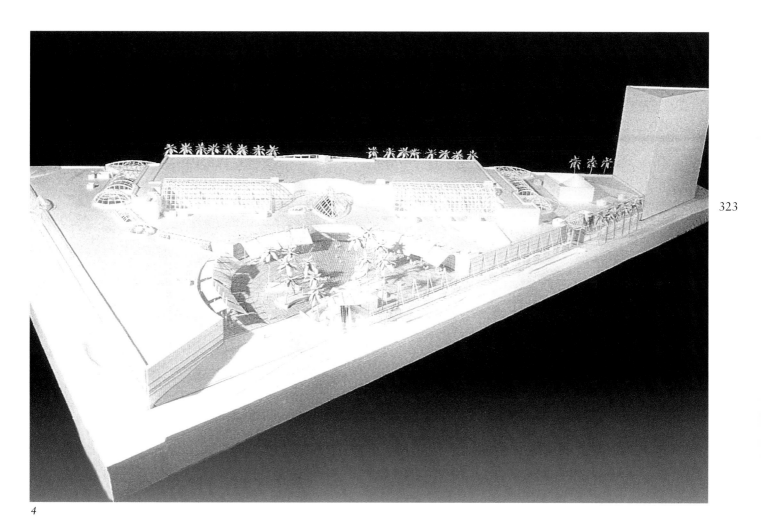

4

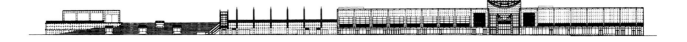

5

6

7

8

9

Cerdà in 1859, and on the soon-to-be-constructed seaward extension of Cerdà's grand boulevard, the Avinguda Diagonal. While we contributed to the master plan developed by an international team assembled by the American developer Gerald Hines, who acquired the prime parcel after two previous development attempts had failed, our principal role was as designer for the three-story entertainment and retail center, which will include Spain's largest "hyper-market" and Europe's largest multiscreen cinema. The retail center seeks to adapt the typical American mall, which is suburban and introspective, to the conditions of a site that aspires to the urbanity of a city center. It looks inward to three-story skylit galleries and outward to the street; shops will open onto what is hoped will soon be active sidewalks and the nearby metro stop along the Avinguda Diagonal, traditionally Barcelona's premier retail address.

Each of the center's three retail levels has a distinct character. The lowest level, with buff-colored limestone piers and wide segmental arches and vaults, recalls a traditional Catalan market and is leased primarily to merchants of food and daily staples; the second level, at grade, with its glass and steel palette and black and white stone paving, caters to fashion and related shops; the top level, with patterned-glass vaulted skylights and outdoor roof terraces opening with views to the adjacent park and to the sea beyond, is the entertainment level, with the cinema and restaurants. Though history is recalled, the spirit of the design is modern and forward-looking, with facades combining crisp glass, steel detailing, and gridded panels of Spanish limestone.

8. Typical Carrer Taulat storefront
9. Typical Avinguda Diagonal storefront
10. Avinguda Diagonal storefront

Preservation and Development Plan

Heiligendamm, Germany
1996–

326 Germany's most historic seaside resort, Heiligendamm is located in the eastern part of the country on the coast of the Baltic Sea, approximately two-hundred kilometers north of Berlin and two-hundred kilometers northeast of Hamburg. Founded in 1793 by Baron Friedrich Franz I as a curative spa, Heiligendamm expanded throughout the nineteenth century when it was a renowned luxury resort known as the "white city by the sea." Early spa buildings around the waterfront square were designed by Berlin neoclassicist Carl Theodor Severin, who was inspired by the English resort architecture of Brighton and Bath. During the Communist era part of the waterfront complex was used as a hospital, while the villas were drastically modified.

Our assignment includes the restoration and adaptive reuse of the historic villas and hotels as well as the development of a new town on 105 hectares facing a new eighteen-hole golf course. The new development is knit carefully into the existing town with a clear hierarchy of roads that encompasses everything from gently curving boulevards to intimate winding residential streets. A wide variety of residences will include attached and detached single-family houses as well as dense apartment buildings near a market square located within walking distance of the train station and the historic resort.

1. *Bird's-eye view*
2. *Waterfront square with existing Kurhaus and Badehaus*
3. *Existing waterfront villas*
4. *View of existing waterfront from pier*

1

2

3

4

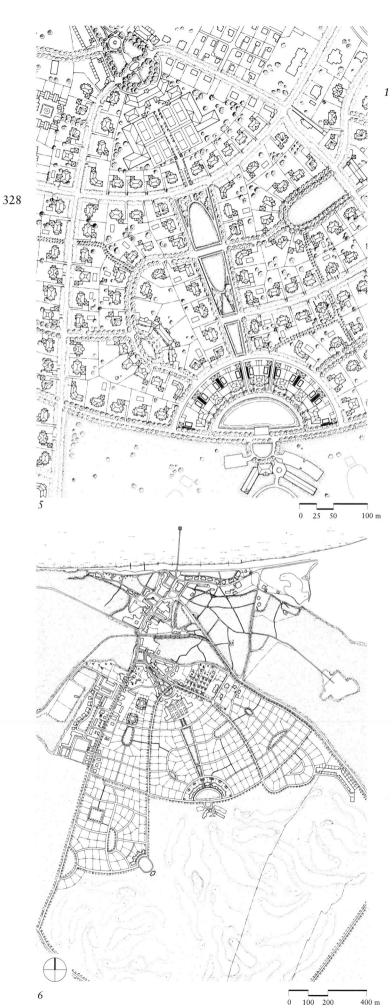

5. *Site plan detail*
6. *Site plan*
7. *Waterfront villas*
8. *Kurhaus and Badehaus elevation*
9. *Grand Hotel elevation*
10. *Haus Seestern elevation*

328

5

0   25   50   100 m

6

0   100   200   400 m

7

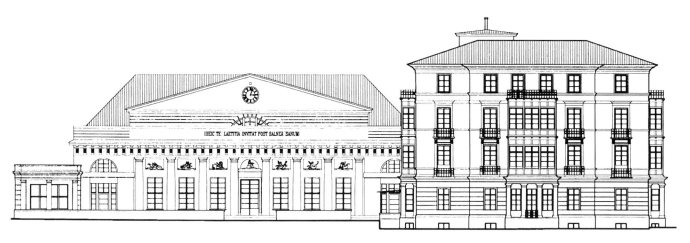

8

9

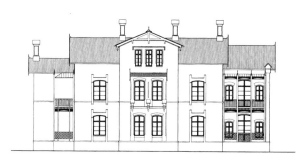

10

Hobby Center for the Performing Arts

Houston, Texas
1996–

330 Comprising the 2,700-seat Sarofim Theater intended for musical productions, a 500-seat black-box theater to serve community groups as well as chamber music, and a performing-arts school, the Hobby Center will replace the functionally outmoded Sam Houston Coliseum and Music Hall (1936). Taking advantage of one of Houston's most prominent downtown sites, facing Tranquility Park and the business district skyline, the dynamically configured colonnade of our design, responding to the irregular site, attempts to bridge the gap in size and artistic ambition between the Art Deco city hall and its bland annex to the south and the vaguely Miesian Albert Thomas Hall to the north. Because the dramatically formed Hobby Center is viewed from all sides, including from above—its roofscape is visible from office buildings—the building is intended to be perceived as three separate copper-roofed buildings. A grandly scaled sixty-foot-high glazed promenade-level lobby unites the composition and confronts the park with a major public room for the city. A covered open-air passageway, dramatically cleaved between the music hall and the school, will help connect downtown with the soon-to-be-enhanced Bayou recreational area while providing a weather-protected setting for outdoor community events.

The design of the Sarofim Theater returns to the pattern established by architects Herts & Tallant in early-twentieth-century New York, creating a festive mood that complements the Broadway-type musical productions that will be showcased. Invoking a gazebo open to the night sky, the cubic volume of the theater brings the audience into close contact with the actors. The second balcony, farther forward than the first, brings far more seats closer to the stage than is typical in so large a theater, while a shallow dome unites the audience in a simple, grandly scaled room.

1. *View across Tranquility Park from east*
2. *Site plan*
3. *Ticketing-level plan*
4. *Orchestra-level plan*

1

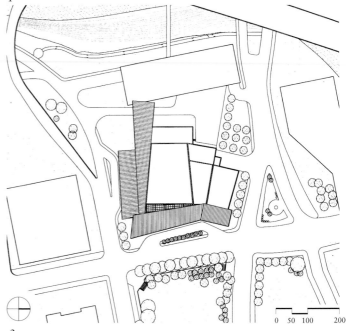

2

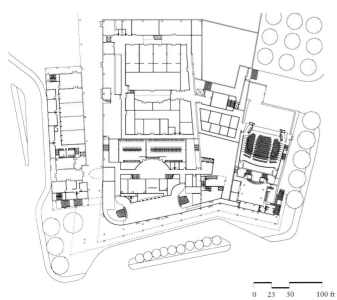

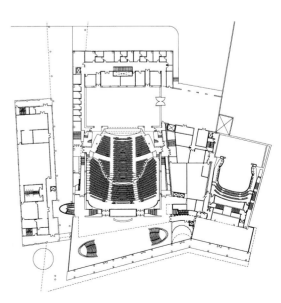

0 25 50   100 ft

3

4

5

6

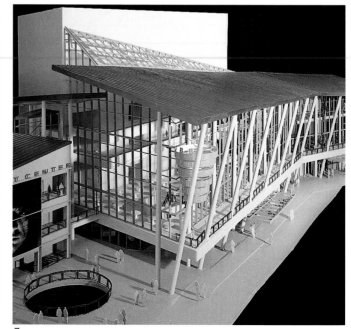

7

5. Southeast facade
6. East facade
7. Orchestra lobby and entrance to
   underground parking
8. South elevation
9. Section through Sarofim Theater and lobby
10. Sarofim Theater
11. Orchestra lobby

10

8

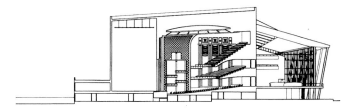

9

11

New York Coliseum Site

New York, New York
1996–1998

1. *Existing site*
2. *Site plan*
3. *Aerial view from east*

334 The site of the thirty-eight-year-old New York Coliseum and Office Building is New York's most contested piece of real estate. In the late 1980s, it was auctioned by the Metropolitan Transportation Authority for one of the highest prices ever paid for a property of its size, but the successful bidder, after having his first scheme trounced by the public, and his second rendered unmarketable by a precipitous collapse of the real-estate market, backed off from the project. Our plan, prepared for the Trump Organization, which entered a new competition to choose a new developer, calls for the demolition of the office tower and its replacement with a 750-foot-high residential tower slab rising from a dramatically reconfigured Coliseum, which would be used for retail and entertainment venues. The tower slab, accommodating apartments and a hotel, complements the towers along Central Park South and Central Park West. Chevronlike setbacks honor the orthogonal geometry of the city's grid; the diagonal placement of the mass on the site reflects similar conditions at the two northern corners of Central Park. A publicly accessible rooftop garden of immense proportions re-creates the New York tradition of elevated outdoor areas, which dates back to the turn of the century and is currently best represented by the roof gardens of Rockefeller Center.

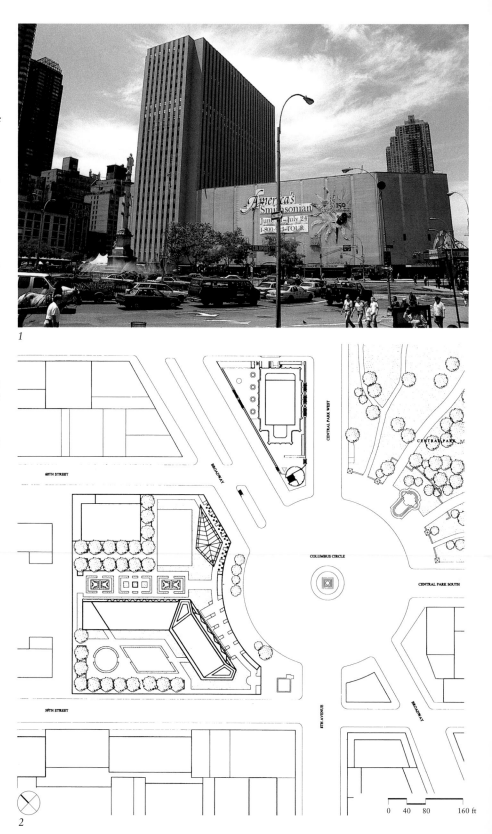

1

2

0 40 80 160 ft

336

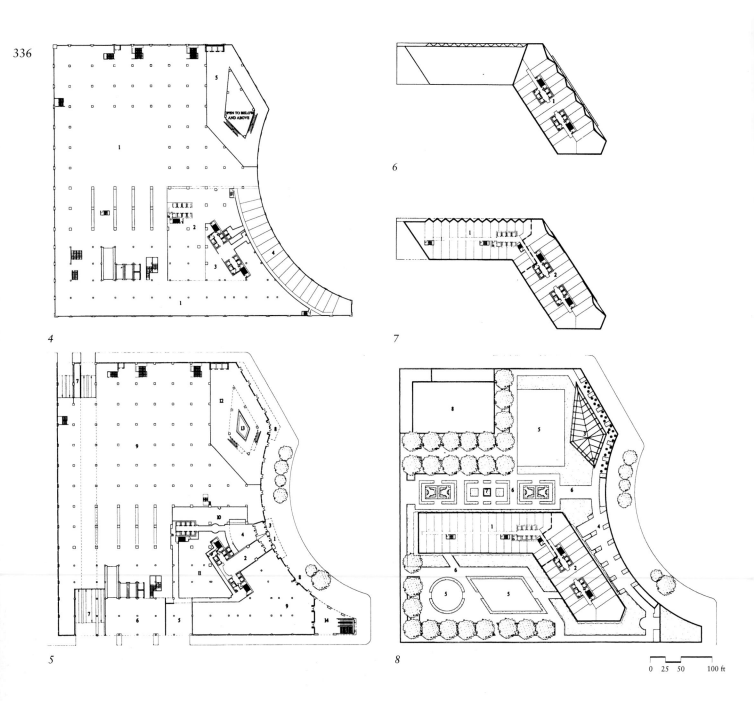

Residence

Mount Kisco, New York
1996

338 The relationship of new buildings to monuments of the modernist past, one of the most challenging problems of current practice, was the central issue here. The glassy, pavilionlike house designed by Edward Larrabee Barnes in 1951 for his own use—a version of Philip Johnson's Glass House in New Canaan, Connecticut—did not easily lend itself to extension, as Barnes himself demonstrated with the two awkward wings he added in the 1970s. Our proposal replaces Barnes's additions with new, boldly shaped wings embracing the original pavilion, which is to be restored.

1. *Entry (south) facade*
2. *Site plan*
3. *Ground-floor plan*

1

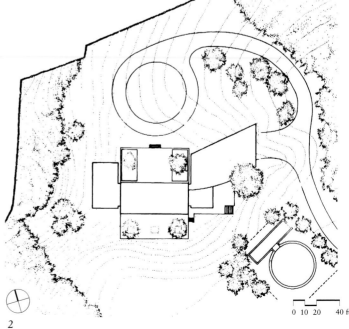

2

0 10 20   40 ft

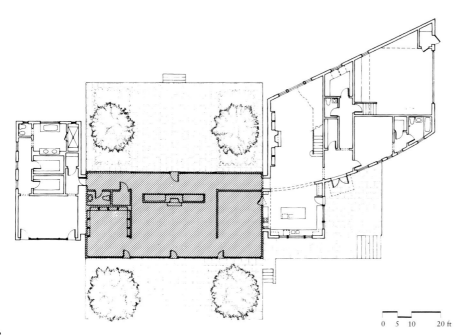

0 5 10 20 ft

3

Guest House and Tennis Pavilion in Brentwood

Los Angeles, California
1996–1998

340 When our clients, for whom we had designed an East Coast summer house, moved west, they invited their architects along to design a guest house and a guard house to complement the forty-year-old Wallace Neff–designed house they purchased. This house was country French in character with an occasional Polynesian eave detail, an acceptable combination in southern California.

Our work included extensive reorganization of the landscape with a formal parterre garden and a fountain. A new gravel-paved court forms the entry to the house and the new guest house, a simple hipped-roof volume detailed in brick and timber. Inside, the ceiling of the screening room, the principal feature of the house, is timbered and trussed and follows the exterior roofline.

1

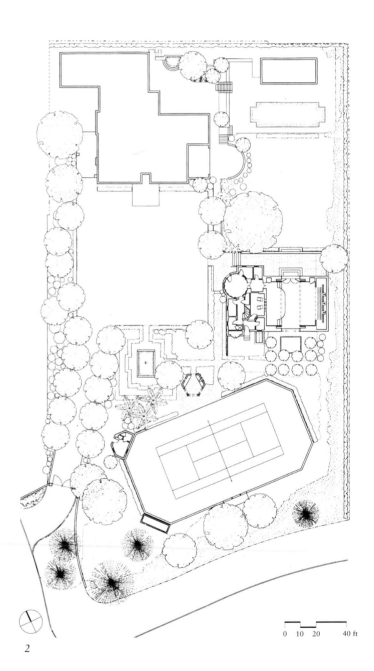

2

0   10   20   40 ft

1. *Existing house*
2. *Site plan*
3. *View of main house and*
   guest house from entry
4. *East elevation of guest house*
5. *North elevation of guest house*

3

4

5

Residence in Napa County

Oakville, California
1996–

342 Our first house in the northern California countryside will occupy a spectacular site where deep ravines and rugged topography combine with vegetation and weather that invoke Tuscany. An informal arrangement of stucco-faced and tile-roofed volumes of various scales roughly corresponds to the individual rooms of the plan, each forming a formal entity in its own right, all suggesting a house built over time.

1. Entry-level plan
2. Site plan
3. South elevation of guest house
   with main house beyond
4. Entry facade from southeast
5. Living room

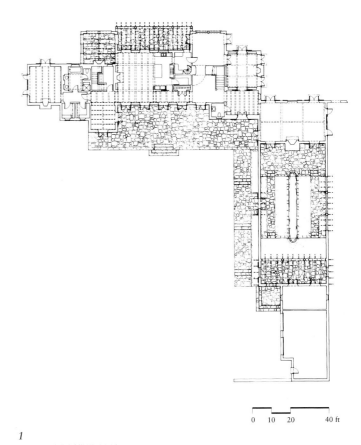

0 10 20   40 ft

1

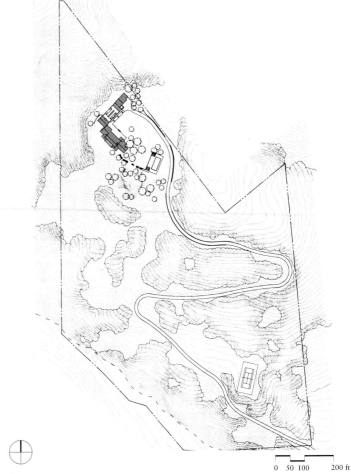

0 50 100   200 ft

2

3

4

5

Residence

Long Island, New York
1997–

344 Our design for this oceanfront villa borrows from French Directoire precedents. Organized around a long two-story mass to which lower service wings are connected by curved hyphens, the scheme forms a square entry court commensurate with the formal symmetry of the massing. On the ocean side, the two-story volume stands alone—the wings receding—to reduce the perceived size of the house and to open up views along the beach as well as out to sea.

The plan arranges the principal formal rooms in an enfilade along the south, while a sequence of broad galleries links informal living and service areas to the east and west. A series of consistently detailed and scaled paneled rooms is relieved at the center of the house by the elliptical double-height stair hall.

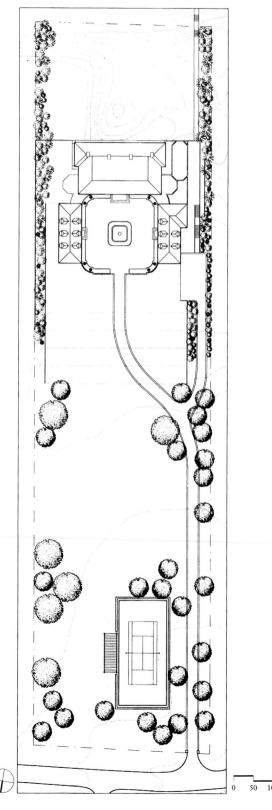

0   50   100   200 ft

1

2

3

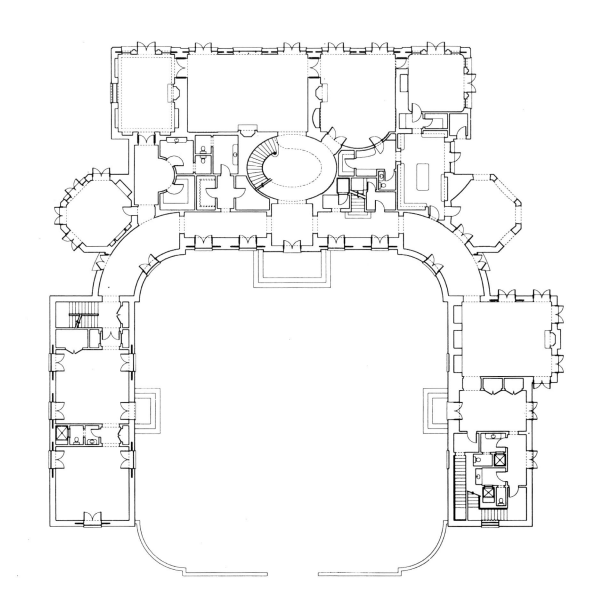

4

0   5   10   20 ft

Edgewater Apartments

West Vancouver,
British Columbia, Canada
1997–1999

346 The massing of this tower, which contains fifteen luxury units—three townhouse apartments at the base, eleven full-floor tower apartments, and a two-story penthouse apartment—responds to street setback and height zoning requirements; the disposition of rooms within each apartment is influenced by the views of English Bay to the south and west and West Vancouver's uplands to the north. The pedimented vault at the roof creates dramatic interior spaces in the penthouse apartment while masking mechanical functions that would otherwise be visible to neighbors on the nearby hillside. At the same time, it helps distinguish the building from its largely unconsidered high-rise neighbors. Construction commenced in the summer of 1998.

3

1

2

0 5 10   20 ft

4

5

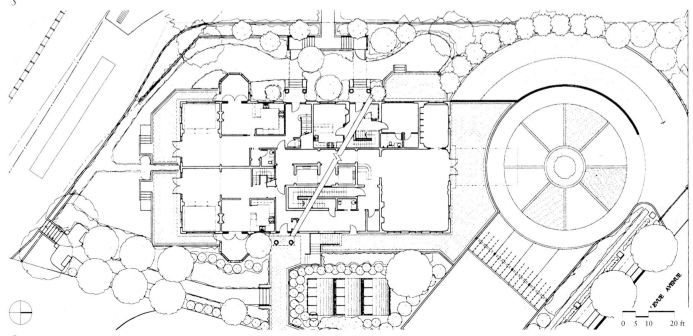

6

Belas Clube de Campo

Lisbon, Portugal
1997–

348 A new suburb on a 326-hectare site that for hundreds of years had been a family-owned country estate combines a town center with residential neighborhoods fitting into a topographically challenging landscape. To separate our community from unsightly uses outside our client's property, a gateway building at the principal point of entrance to the site forms the edge of a well-defined town square. From here a clear hierarchy of roads, including straight wide boulevards, winding parkways, and narrow, intimate residential streets, reaches out to archipelagos of residential development that enjoy spectacular views down natural valleys permanently dedicated as open space.

0 100 200   400 m

1

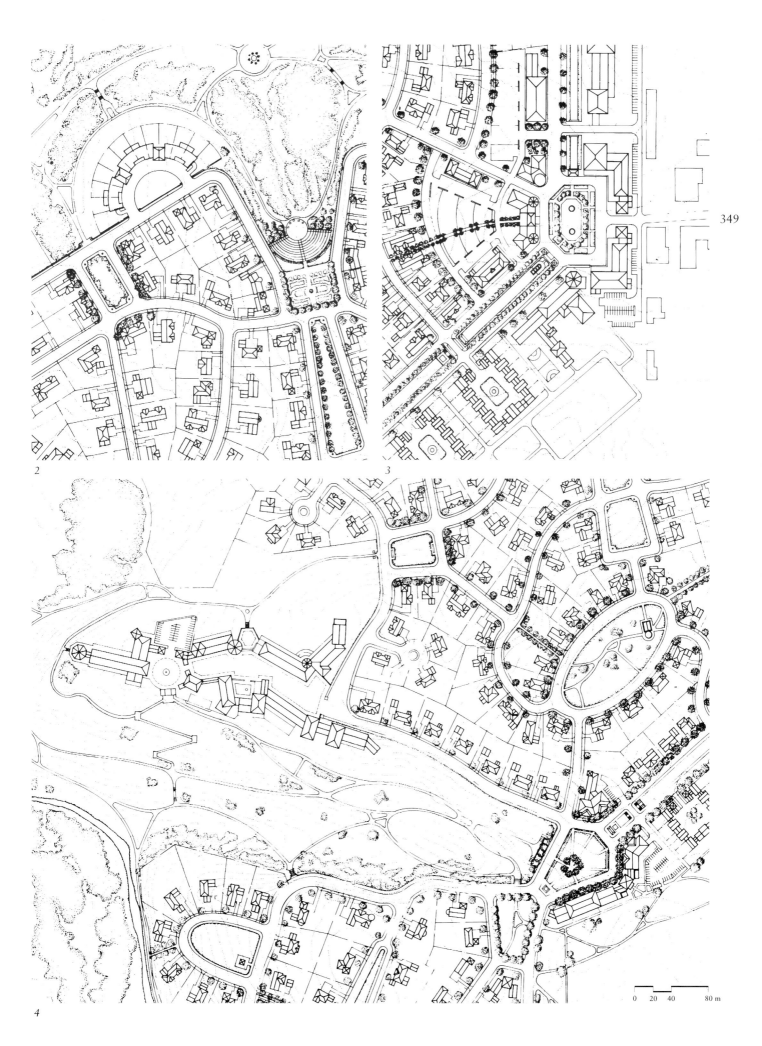

2

3

4

0 20 40 80 m

5

6

5. *View of apartment buildings along ridge*
6. *View of neighborhood park*
7. *View along canal street*

Welcome Center,
Give Kids the World

Kissimmee, Florida
1997–

1. *Garden facade*
2. *Ground-floor plan*
3. *Entry*
4. *Garden elevation*
5. *Site plan*

352   Give Kids the World, which provides terminally ill children and their families a dream-come-true vacation at the theme parks of the Orlando area, occupies a campus that includes residences, dining facilities, and entertainment venues, all designed to comfort and entertain sick children, the guests of honor. Our reception center is the point of transition between the real world and the extremely thematic and child-oriented buildings within the compound. Welcoming and orienting, it caters to families who are very troubled, icing spaces devoted to schedule-planning and other routine vacation functions with whimsy while, we hope, avoiding condescension.

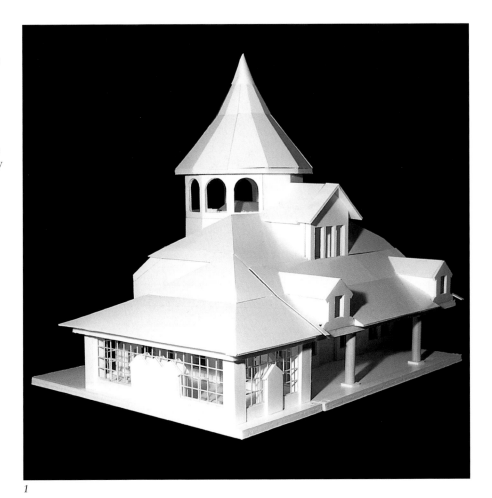

1

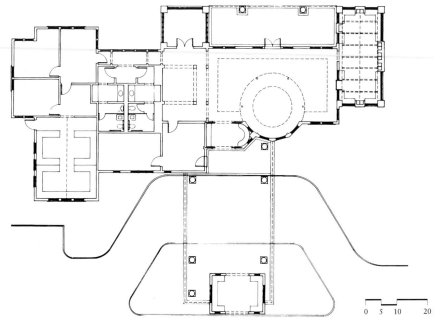

2

0   5   10   20 ft

3

4

5

0   25   50   100 ft

Tuxedo Reserve

Tuxedo, New York
1997–

354   The master plan and guidelines for the new community of Tuxedo Reserve are informed by the site's complicated terrain and the specific architectural traditions of the region, especially that of the adjacent, hundred-year-old planned community of Tuxedo Park. Unlike that development, ours has not been conceived as a rich man's hunting preserve but as a year-round community for average homeowners.

Our plan proposes a series of neighborhoods grouped around public amenities such as neighborhood greens and community facilities. A small hamlet with tree-lined streets, community parks, and mixed-use and civic buildings will create a strong center. Buildings are clustered as much as possible to maintain the integrity of the land, approximately three-quarters of which is preserved in its natural state. Each neighborhood will contain a variety of housing sizes and types in order to embrace the variety typical of real towns as opposed to the homogeneity of typical suburban subdivisions.

An integral part of our work is the preparation of guidelines intended to direct the long-term future development of the community. Hundreds of detailed decisions are involved, from the treatment of road edges to the level of night lighting, from paving materials to construction density and how this density is distributed throughout the site. For most residents, probably the most important and most easily perceived measure of the development's character will be the architecture of the buildings, especially their sympathetic relationship to each other and to the land. Therefore our goal is to foster a community of buildings that together are more than the sum of their parts. Tuxedo Park, Tuxedo Hamlet, and Sloatsburg, as well as the historic Hudson River towns with their difficult, steep topography, have much to teach us. They form the background of our work, contributing an extra dimension to our approach and leading us to a solution that is not only specific to the site but also to the historic region as a whole.

1. *South Village*
2. *Gatehouse*
3. *Apartment court*
4. *Town center site plan*

1

2

3

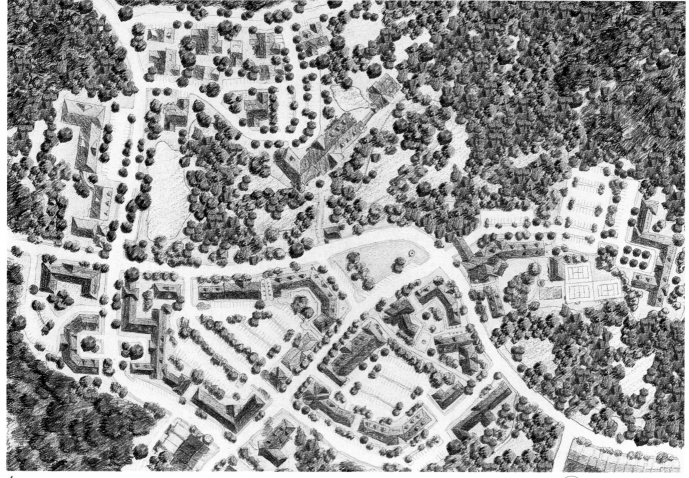

4

Maharani Menari Tower

Jakarta, Indonesia
1997

1. *Typical tower plan*
2. *Typical base plan*
3. *Site plan*
4. *View from Galunggung Street*

356 Located at the edge of a loosely organized office and commercial development area, our building, one of a proposed twin-tower development, refers in its articulation and in its planning strategies to the clarity and order that Western architecture brought to Jakarta in an earlier time. Recent speculative development in Jakarta has created a sprawling megalopolis with little to distinguish one office park or residential development from another. Our return to an earlier era of design was not arbitrary or capricious: many local and international observers of the Jakarta scene have strong respect and pride for the classically inspired historic heart of the city. In planning this tower, the classicism makes symbolic as well as practical sense: the arcaded base provides sun and rain protection at the shopping level; the unencumbered floor plans permit flexible interior planning that also yields special conditions for executive offices, conference rooms, and the like. At the crown, an iconic and memorable pavilion that can be seen from great distances will mark the location of the development and, perhaps, a call to order. The present economic crisis has put the project on hold.

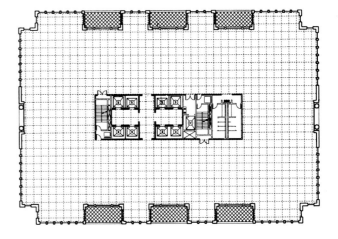

1

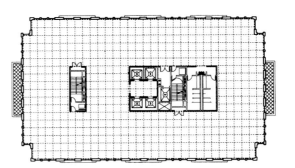

2

0 2.5 5   10 m

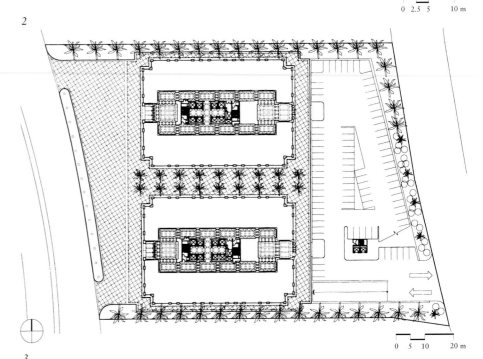

3

0 5 10   20 m

Trump St. Moritz Condominiums

New York, New York
1997

1. Original design by Emery Roth (1929)
2. View from Central Park
3. French balcony detail
4. Ground-floor plan
5. Central Park South elevation

358   Two factors justify this project, which calls for the recladding of Emery Roth's Italianate 1929 St. Moritz Hotel: the structural instability of the existing brick walls, which have long been neglected, and the need to create fewer and much larger windows to coincide with the transformation of the interior plan from one of small, virtually identical hotel rooms to one of large apartments. No change to the massing was permitted. Our proposed new facade, gesturing to the stylish modern classicism of the 1930s with abstract details in the cast stone and the metal trim, was intended as a contextual response to neighbors, especially Mayer & Whittlesey's 40 Central Park South (1941) next door and the glamorous trio of hotels on the next block—the Barbizon, Hampshire House, and Essex House. Preservationists preferred a different approach that incorporated fragments of Roth's ornament in an imitation of the original. Then the building's owners switched developers and the project was abandoned.

1

2

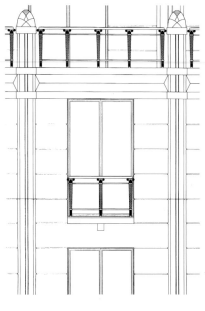

3

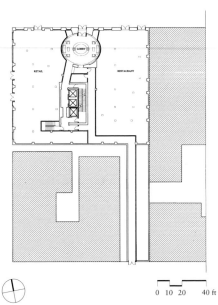

4

0 10 20   40 ft

Office Building and Parking Garage

Yonkers, New York
1997–

360   An important first step toward the realization of a master plan for the revitalization of the city's long-dormant downtown, this project combines an architecturally enhanced six-hundred-car parking garage with a contextually responsive thirty-thousand-square-foot retail and office building facing Main Street. Also included are six townhouses containing twelve apartments for moderate-income families at the rear of the site, facing the established residential neighborhood along Hudson Street.
The bold scale of our curving facade is in keeping with the key location of the office building opposite the train station and post office, where it will form a gateway to downtown.

1. *Existing conditions along Hudson Street*
2. *View from train station toward Main Street retail and office space*
3. *Third-level plan*
4. *View of townhouses and parking along Hudson Street*
5. *View of Main Street retail and office space*

1

2

3

0   20   40   80 ft

4

5

Residence at Maidstone

East Hampton, New York
1997–1999

362   Sited on the second dune, this house
will enjoy panoramic views of the sea,
the adjacent golf course, and, to the north
across Hook Pond, the historic village.
The open dunescape suggested a low-
profile mass articulated with dormers
and porches set below the ridge.
The downhill slope of the site allows
the entry to be set a full half-level below
the main floor, giving rise to a grander
entry sequence than might be expected
in so low-slung a composition.

1. Site plan
2. Main-floor plan
3. Perspective of entry facade
4. Perspective of ocean facade

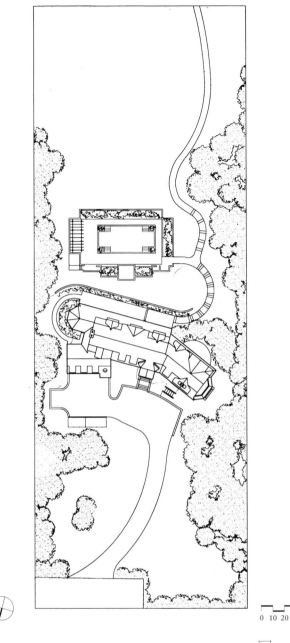

1

0 10 20   40 ft

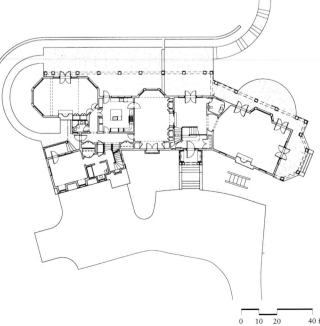

2

0 10 20   40 ft

3

4

Apartment Tower at Sixty-Fifth Street and Third Avenue

New York, New York
1997–2000

364   This 206,000-square-foot, 32-story tower on Manhattan's Upper East Side will house 149 apartments, with a distribution of five apartments on a typical floor and one to two apartments on upper floors. Although the tower-on-base massing reflects New York's current zoning, the red-brick and limestone facades, articulated with French balconies, bay windows, and subtle changes in plane, recall highly respected luxury apartment buildings of the 1920s and 1930s, such as those located along Park Avenue. The top of the building consists of a series of setbacks culminating in a lantern, intended as a notable addition to the city's skyline.

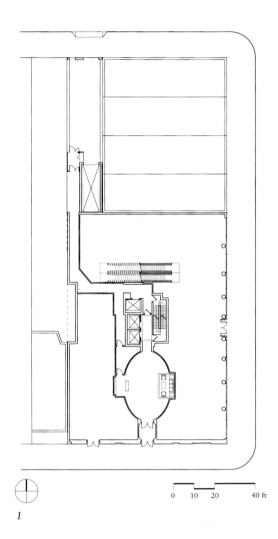

1. Ground-floor plan
2. View looking up Third Avenue

1

RiverVue

Tuckahoe, New York
1997–

366   Our contribution to the redevelopment of
a ten-acre site straddling the Bronx River
includes the restoration of a historic mill,
which will be part of a restaurant
complex overlooking the river, as well
as the design of a recreation pavilion
and thirteen two-story single-family
villas located along the river's edge.
To provide architectural variety and
also to accommodate different site
conditions, there will be four villa types.
A vocabulary of low-pitched roofs with
wide, overhanging eaves and pergolas
combines with the spare use of trim to
create a coherent ensemble of reasonably
varied components.

1. *View of villas from clubhouse*
2. *View of site across Bronx River from south*
3. *Site plan*

1

2

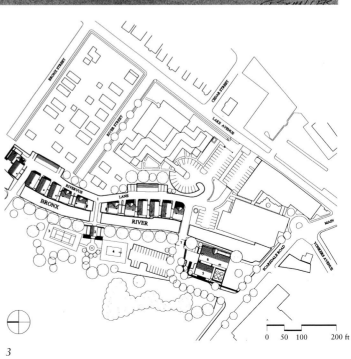

The Seville

New York, New York
1997–

368   With its light-colored brick facade and black columnar-brick accents, this 31-story, 170-unit apartment tower is an interpretation of New York's towerlike hotel and apartment buildings of the late-1920s and 1930s. Those structures, with an emphasis on simple shapes and verticality combined with corner windows and increased areas of glass, adapted skyscraper typologies for urban living for the first time.

1. *Residential lobby*
2. *Residential lobby*
3. *Ground-floor plan*
4. *View looking down Second Avenue*

1

2

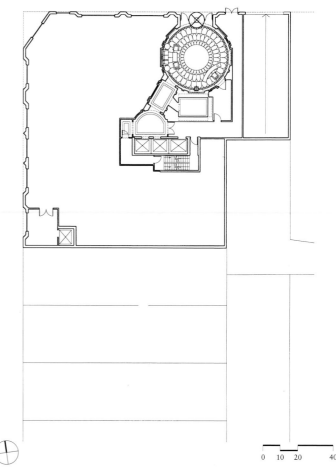

0   10   20   40 ft

3

South Station

Boston, Massachusetts
1997

1. View of lobby winter garden
2. Site plan
3. View from northwest

370 With the reconstruction of the Central Artery and the renewed vitality of the financial district, the land behind South Station, too long isolated from Boston's downtown business district, is ripe for redevelopment. The competition program called for a phased development that would begin with an 850-foot-high office tower, which would be followed by a 600-room hotel and a smaller office building.

Our design featured an octagonal office tower intended as a highly identifiable landmark, not only visible but, by virtue of its geometric regularity, identifiable from an almost infinite variety of vantage points. In its massing, design, and detailing, the tower draws upon the time-honored principles of traditional skyscraper design. In no way is our tower to be confused with the superficially ornamented boxes typical of Boston's 1980s skyscraper boom; ours is a classical interweave of strong vertical structural piers with overlapping large- and small-scale window-wall grids. To enhance the tower's sculptural effect, eight corners rise vertically from the base while the eight glassy faces between them slope gently inward as the tower rises—giving the shaft a subtle classical entasis and at the same time maintaining a relatively constant depth as the core diminishes toward the top. Minor set-backs articulate the vertical composition and ease the transition between the vertical shaft and the low-lying station in front of it.

A glass-roofed great room mediates between the historic station and the tower, forming a light-filled place that would become a monumental crossroads. At night the crystalline roof above the great room would glow like a lantern, brilliantly marking the terminus of the new park that will cover the rebuilt Central Artery while announcing the civic space within.

1

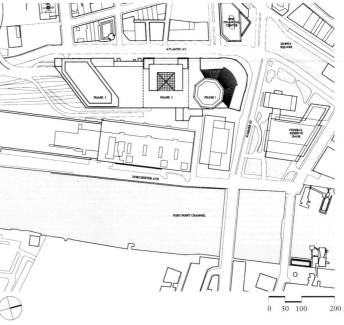

2

0   50 100   200 ft

3

Senior Community

Celebration, Florida
1997–

372 In every way possible, this senior community seeks to extend the planning and architecture of Celebration as a whole. Two-story villas housing the most mobile residents continue the scale of adjacent residential neighborhoods. A large central building, containing apartments for the less mobile residents as well as the bulk of the community functions, is fragmented in plan so that from a resident's point of view it appears to be made up of many different buildings defining a series of outdoor courts. Inside, a grand triple-height lobby living room serves as the focus of myriad function rooms, including the dining room and the south-facing glass-enclosed swimming pool.

1. *Aerial view from south*
2. *Entrance court*
3. *Entry drive*

1

2

Animation and Emerging Technologies Building, Sheridan College

*Oakville-Trafalgar,
Ontario, Canada
1997*

374   Sheridan College's Oakville Campus comprises a group of nondescript buildings loosely arranged around an open-ended landscaped courtyard. Our response to the solicitation of proposals from teams of architects and developers for a new consolidated facility offered a sixty-thousand-square-foot building, to be realized in stages, that would close the leaky space of the courtyard and have as its principal feature a sixty-foot-high canopy marking the entrance. Another team, offering a richer financial deal for the college, was selected.

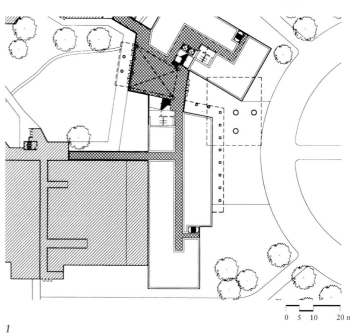

0   5   10   20 m

1

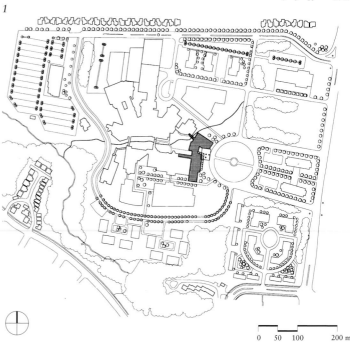

0   50   100   200 m

2

3

4

5

Arts Center, Denison University

Granville, Ohio
1998–

376   An eighty-two-thousand-square-foot facility, consisting principally of a four-hundred-seat theater, a four-thousand-square foot black-box theater, and an art gallery, is intended to unite daily two different areas of the campus and two different constituencies of the Denison community: the academic buildings on the heights and the arts building sixty feet below where the campus meets the town. The new building will complement the ninety-year-old Cleveland Hall, originally a gymnasium and now home to the school's painting studios. Our competition design rides the crest of the hill, grouping various functions along a grand stair that passes to one side, where large windows open to spacious views and, from the outside, give glimpses of the activity within. The stair and its landings form part of the art gallery, making changing exhibits part of the daily journey. The theaters share lobby space located off a terrace directly behind Cleveland Hall, where broad steps welcome the town to performances.

The materials and massing of the arts center, gesturing to the historic buildings on the heights, combine limestone and brick walls with simple gable and hip roofs. Where the building faces away from the traditional campus and can be seen from great distances, we utilize steel columns and large glazed areas, which present a bolder scale and more open character. The stagehouse and theater volumes are embedded in the hillside and are surrounded by smaller program elements to minimize the building's overall impact on the landscape.

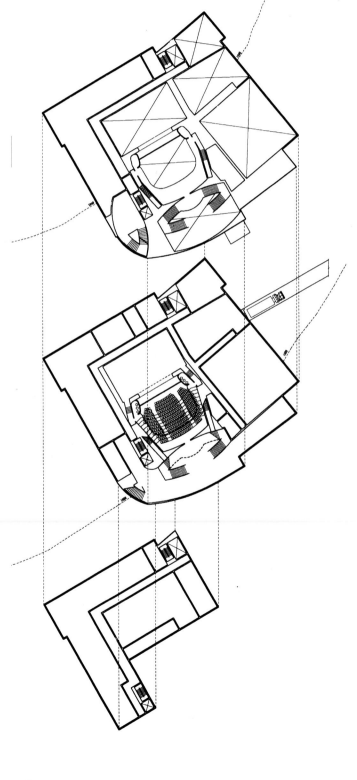

1

2

0   40   80   160 ft

3

4

Residence

Palo Alto, California
1998–

378 This Palladian-inspired residence is located in a neighborhood known locally as Old Palo Alto. Though the surrounding housing stock is stylistically diverse, the prevalent style is Italianate; thus the palette of materials—stucco, stone, and tile roof—is familiar to the area. The L configuration of the house and pool allows the principal interior and exterior spaces to enjoy a southern exposure and views toward hundred-year-old California live oaks that line the southern edge of the half-acre site.

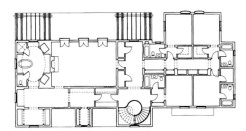

1

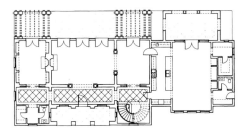

2

0 5 10   20 ft

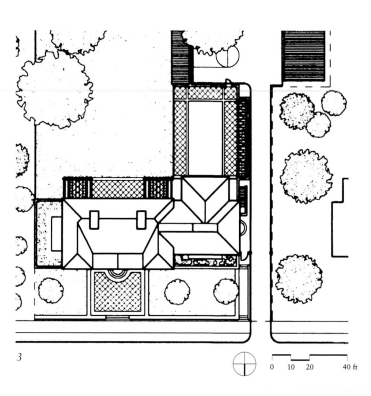

3

0   10   20   40 ft

4

5

6

7

House for
This Old House Magazine

Wilton, Connecticut
1998–1999

380   The design and construction of this 5,500-square-foot house, which will be lived in by the builder and his family, will be documented in *This Old House* magazine. The placement of the house on the northern edge of a rolling open site demarked by fieldstone walls, where it will provide panoramic views from the major rooms and porch, requires that the entrance be at the back. The rambling character of the massing breaks down the scale of the house and forms the circle of the entry courtyard, giving the appearance that the house has grown slowly and naturally over time as it has settled comfortably into its site.

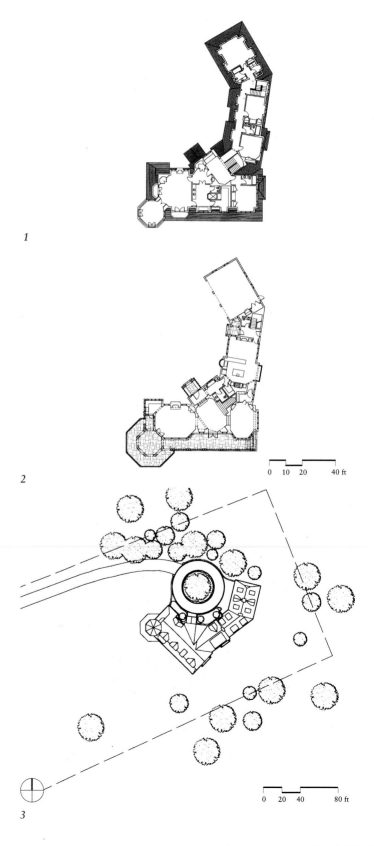

1

2

0   10   20   40 ft

3

0   20   40   80 ft

4

5

Reforma 350

Mexico City, Mexico
1998–1999

382 Our design for a nineteen-story office building on Mexico City's prestigious Paseo de la Reforma strips a banal and clumsily detailed precast-concrete-clad building of the early 1980s to its structure and then resculpts and reclads it, turning an aggressively serrated mass into a series of layered, glass surfaces complementing the city's landmark monument to the Angel of Mexican Independence. The outermost layer of our design, a gently scalloped glass curtain, rises from the street to an eighteenth-floor balcony, orienting the building toward the monument and announcing the building's relocated main entrance below. At the street level this new entrance, flanked by continuously glazed shopfronts, opens onto a widened sidewalk. Above the street level, five floors of parking receive natural ventilation through a screen of layered, structurally glazed, glass "shingles." An openwork metal cornice at the top of the building visually terminates the facade while concealing window-washing equipment.

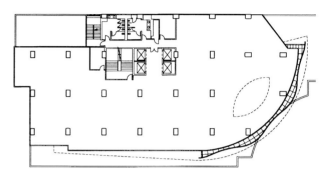

2

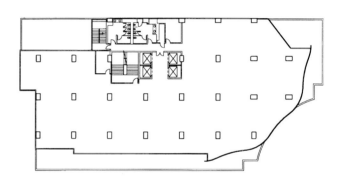

3

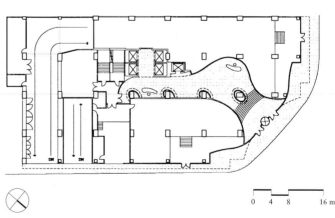

4

0 4 8   16 m

1

Public Library of Nashville and Davidson County

Nashville, Tennessee
1998–2001

384   Nashville is "Music City USA"; it is also, and has been for much longer, the "Athens of the South," with a strong, distinct classical tradition that permeates its architecture, from William Strickland's Tennessee State Capitol to modest houses in the many residential neighborhoods. Our library recognizes that tradition, not only in its exterior massing and formal language but in the clear, axial organization of its most symbolically significant public areas—the main entry lobby; the Nashville Room, housing the local history collection; the gallery; the great reading room; the skylit grand stair; and the garden courtyard—all of which are located on the axis of the capitol, helping to strengthen the dangerously frayed fabric of the civic center complex.

We strongly believe libraries are primarily social places where information and knowledge can be found. People come to libraries to see and interact with other people as well as to acquire knowledge. The main spaces of our design are uniquely suited to this interaction, from the grand figural spaces for reading and circulation to the quiet eddies of informal seating that are distributed throughout the open stack areas, especially around the courtyard. Our building is functional and grand; it is definitely not a shopping mall for books.

1. *North-south section*
2. *Perspective view of Church Street facade*
3. *Ground-level plan*
4. *Second-level plan*
5. *Third-level plan*

2

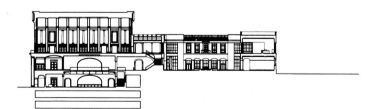

1

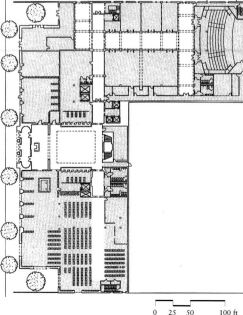

0   25   50   100 ft

3

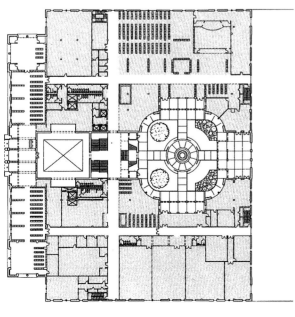

4

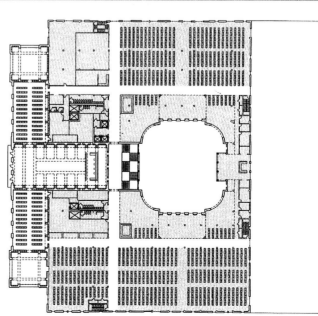

5

The three-story height along Church Street was derived from a practical desire to retain the existing parking structure; we took advantage of its structural capacity to locate above it two large floors that look outward to the surrounding townscape and inward to a landscaped courtyard. The courtyard, with its central fountain, pool, and covered arcade, will provide an oasis and a setting for special readings and events.

6

7

6. Detail of Church Street facade
7. Courtyard
8. View from Tennessee State Capitol

9

10

9. *Entry hall*
10. *Stair hall*
11. *Great reading room*

Project Information

390 **Architects' Office**
New York, New York, 1994–1995

Project Associate: Augusta Barone. Assistants: Carolyn Straub, Lynn Wang.

Center for Jewish Life, Princeton University
Princeton, New Jersey, 1986–1993

Associate Partner: Alexander P. Lamis. Schematic Design Phase Associate: Thomas A. Kligerman. Senior Assistants: Lee Ledbetter (design); Preston Gumberich (construction administration). Assistants: Stephen T. B. Falatko, Alexis O. Fernandez, Abigail M. Huffman, Valerie Hughes, Arthur Platt, Pat Tiné, Elizabeth A. Valella.

"For Architect Robert Stern, Center for Jewish Life Is Small, but Tough, Project," *Princeton Today*, spring 1988, 7.

Eric Thompson, "Building a Better University," *Nassau*, October 17, 1991, 10–11.

Philip Arcidi, "Projects: Filling in Princeton," *Progressive Architecture*, April 1992, 127–29.

Robert A. M. Stern: Buildings and Projects, 1987–1992, with an introduction by Vincent Scully (New York: Rizzoli, 1992), 312–13.

Robert A. M. Stern: Buildings (New York: The Monacelli Press, 1996), 358–69.

Spruce Lodge
Colorado, 1987–1991

Architect in Charge, Design and Construction Documents: Thomas A. Kligerman. Associate Partner, Construction: Arthur Chabon. Assistants: Silvina Goefron, Timothy Haines, Abigail Huffman, Valerie Hughes, Robert Miller, Warren Van Wees. Interiors Associate: Raúl Morillas. Interiors Assistant: Kim Neuscheler. Project Assistant, Bridge and Barn: Roxana I. Klein. Interiors Assistants: Nancy Boszhardt, Deborah Emery, Stephan Johnson, Scott Sloat. Landscape Associate: Robert Ermerins. Landscape Assistant: William C. Skelsey.

The American Houses of Robert A. M. Stern, with an introduction by Clive Aslet (New York: Rizzoli, 1991), 196–99.

Robert A. M. Stern: Houses (New York: The Monacelli Press, 1997), 526–55.

Norman Rockwell Museum at Stockbridge
Stockbridge, Massachusetts, 1987–1993

Architect in Charge: William T. Georgis. Project Associate: Augusta Barone. Assistants: Silvina Goefron, Michelle Huot, Michael D. Jones, Robert Miller, Derrick Smith, Edward H. A. Tuck, Elizabeth A. Valella. Landscape Associate: Robert Ermerins. Senior Landscape Assistants: Laura Schoenbaum, William Skelsey. Landscape Assistant: Charlotte M. Frieze.

Derek Gentile, "Rockwell Museum Board Names New York Architect to Design Linwood Gallery," *Berkshire Eagle*, February 6, 1988, B:9.

Charles Bonenti, "A New Rockwell Museum: Designing for a Legend," *Berkshire Eagle*, February 7, 1988, F:2.

Joseph Giovannini, "Currents: A New England Look for Norman Rockwell," *New York Times*, March 24, 1988, 3:3.

"Berkshire Classical: Stern Wins Norman Rockwell Museum Competition," *Architectural Record*, April 1988, 61.

"Design: Stern Wins Limited Competition for Norman Rockwell Museum," *Architecture*, April 1988, 44.

John Morris Dixon, "P/A News Report: Stern Wins Rockwell Museum," *Progressive Architecture*, April 1988, 25–26.

"File of Architect: Robert A. M. Stern Architects, 1983–1987," *AT Architecture*, November 1988, 26.

Laurie Shaw, "Construction Phase Drawing Near for the New $7.2 Million Norman Rockwell Museum," *Berkshire Business Journal*, May 1990, 3.

Derek Gentile, "Rockwell Architect Plans 'Country Museum,'" *Berkshire Eagle*, June 18, 1990, 2:1, 2.

"New Museum for Rockwell," *New York Times*, May 12, 1991, 10:8.

Robert A. M. Stern: Buildings and Projects, 1987–1992, with an introduction by Vincent Scully (New York: Rizzoli, 1992), 240–41.

"A Shrine to Rockwell's America," *New York Times*, January 21, 1993, C:3.

Robert Campbell, "A Home for Rockwell's World," *Boston Globe*, April 2, 1993, 85, 96.

Lawrence J. Goodrich, "New Rockwell Museum Opens," *Christian Science Monitor*, April 2, 1993, Arts:1ff.

Derek Gentile, "A Museum Warming: Stockbridge Pays Tribute to a Neighbor," *Berkshire Eagle*, April 4, 1993, A:1, 9.

Jerry Adler, "America, America: Norman Rockwell Secures a Place in Art History—His Very Own New Museum," *Newsweek*, April 12, 1993, 58, 59.

William Grimes, "On Picture-Perfect Day, a Norman Rockwell Museum Opens," *New York Times*, June 13, 1993, 1, 34.

Justin Henderson, "An American Classic," *Interiors*, September 1993, 90–93.

Robert A. M. Stern: Buildings (New York: The Monacelli Press, 1996), 318–27.

Residence in River Oaks
Houston, Texas, 1988–1992

Partner: Roger H. Seifter. Project Associate: John Berson. Assistants: Gary Brewer, Abigail Huffman, Kristin McMahon, Daniel Romualdez, Olivia Rowan, Elizabeth A. Valella. Interiors Associate: Raúl Morillas. Interiors Assistants: Pat Burns Ross, Alice Yiu. Landscape Associate: Robert Ermerins. Landscape Assistants: Charlotte M. Frieze, Laura Schoenbaum. Associate Architect: Richard Fitzgerald and Associates.

The American Houses of Robert A. M. Stern, with an introduction by Clive Aslet (New York: Rizzoli, 1991), 62–67.

Robert A. M. Stern: Buildings and Projects, 1987–1992, with an introduction by Vincent Scully (New York: Rizzoli, 1992), 294–97.

Robert A. M. Stern: Houses (New York: The Monacelli Press, 1997), 372–95.

Columbus Regional Hospital
Columbus, Indiana, 1988–1995

Partner: Graham S. Wyatt. Project Manager, Phase I: Barbara Austin Brown. Project Manager, Phase II: Diane Scott. Assistants: Ferenc Annus, Thomas Gay, Preston Gumberich, Timothy E. Lenahan, Sandra L. Parsons, Eva Pohlen, Mary Ellen Stenger, Elizabeth Thompson, Paul Thompson, Pat Tiné. Interiors Associate: Lisa Maurer. Interiors Assistants: Pat Burns Ross, Alice Yiu. Landscape Associates: Robert Ermerins, Charlotte M. Frieze. Landscape Assistants: William Skelsey, Ann Stokes. Associate Architect: Falick/Klein Partnership, Inc.

Susan Ehlers, "Hospital Expanding into 21st Century," *Republic* (Columbus, Indiana), November 20, 1989, 1, 5.

Susan Ehlers, "Hospital Digs into the Future," *Republic* (Columbus, Indiana,) April 6, 1990, 1.

"Hoosier Patron: Cummins Engine Foundation Continues to Foster Design in Columbus, Indiana," *Architecture*, December 1990, 41.

"Robert A. M. Stern," *Newsline* (Columbia University), December 1990–January 1991, 6.

William A. Orth, "Bartholomew County Hospital Undergoes Radical Surgery," *Construction Digest*, March 4, 1991, 16–18.

Susan Ehlers, "Prognosis: On Time, On Budget," *Republic* (Columbus, Indiana), October 23, 1991, 1.

Robert A. M. Stern: Buildings and Projects, 1987–1992, with an introduction by Vincent Scully (New York: Rizzoli, 1992), 270–73.

Clifford A. Pearson, "Columbus Regional Hospital," *Architectural Record*, November 1995, 100–103.

Eleanor Lynn Nesmith, *Health Care Architecture: Designs for the Future* (Washington: AIA Press, 1995), 76–79.

Robert A. M. Stern: Buildings (New York: The Monacelli Press, 1996), 284–303.

Town Square—Wheaton
Wheaton, Illinois, 1988–1992

Partner: Graham S. Wyatt. Senior Assistant: Nancy K. Jordan. Assistants: Tom Eisele, Timothy Haines, Sandra L. Parsons, Paul Thomson.

Michael J. P. Smith, "Robert Stern Vs. Wayne's World," *Inland Architect*, July–August 1990, 20, 22.

Jerry C. Davis, "Wheaton Getting 'Town Square' Mall," *Chicago Sun-Times*, February 4, 1991, 32.

"Town Square Spotlights Specialty Retailers," *Chain Store Age Executive*, November 1991, 50.

David Young, "Shopping Takes Step into the Future," *Chicago Tribune*, March 2, 1992, 19:1, 5.

Robert Sharoff, "It Takes a Stern Hand to Be Whimsical," *DNR*, March 23, 1992, 28.

Neil Stern, "It's Not a Strip Center, Not a Regional Mall," *Crain's Chicago Business*, April 6, 1992, 2:18.

Robert Bruegmann, "Vox Populi," *Inland Architect*, November–December 1992, 52–61.

Robert A. M. Stern: Buildings and Projects, 1987–1992, with an introduction by Vincent Scully (New York: Rizzoli, 1992), 351.

Robert A. M. Stern: Buildings (New York: The Monacelli Press, 1996), 272–79.

Roger Tory Peterson Institute
Jamestown, New York, 1989–1993

Architect in Charge, Design and Construction Documents Phases: William T. Georgis. Partner, Construction Phase: Roger H. Seifter. Project Associates: Laurie D. Kerr, Lynn Wang. Assistants: Ferenc Annus, Augusta Barone, Yvonne Galindo, Silvina Goefron, Abigail M. Huffman, Arthur Platt, Paul Thompson, Elizabeth A. Valella. Landscape Associate: Robert Ermerins. Landscape Assistants: Charlotte M. Frieze, Laura Schoenbaum, William Skelsey.

Robert A. M. Stern: Buildings and Projects, 1987–1992, with an introduction by Vincent Scully (New York: Rizzoli, 1992), 306–9.

Carl Herko, "A Heavenly Haven for Bird-Watchers," *Buffalo News*, May 10, 1994, B:1.

Mildred Schmertz, "Rustic Traditions," *Architecture*, November 1994, 90–97.

Robert A. M. Stern: Buildings (New York: The Monacelli Press, 1996), 338–57.

Anglebrook Golf Club
Somers, New York, 1989–1998

Associate Partner: Grant Marani. Senior Assistants: Joseph Andriola,

Gary Brewer, Amy Dobbs, Carolyn Foug. Assistants: Dino Marcantonio, Lisa Shire, Lynn Wang. Interiors Associate: Pat Burns Ross. Interiors Assistants: Peter Fleming, Fawn Galli.

Robert A. M. Stern: Buildings and Projects, 1987–1992, with an introduction by Vincent Scully (New York: Rizzoli, 1992), 349.

House at Apaquogue
East Hampton, New York, 1989–1993

Associate Partner: Randy M. Correll. Senior Assistant: Daniel Romualdez. Assistant: Gary Brewer. Landscape Associates: Robert Ermerins, Charlotte M. Frieze.

Robert A. M. Stern: Buildings and Projects, 1987–1992, with an introduction by Vincent Scully (New York: Rizzoli, 1992), 322–23.

Nicholas Shrady, "An American Beauty: Colonial Profile for an East Hampton Residence," *Architectural Digest*, December 1995, 160–65, 201.

Robert A. M. Stern: Houses (New York: The Monacelli Press, 1997), 584–605.

Kiawah Beach Club
Kiawah Island, South Carolina, 1989–1994

Partner: Roger H. Seifter. Project Associate: John Berson. Senior Assistant: Robert Epley. Assistants: Charles Brainerd, Michael Granville, Michael Jacobs.

Robert A. M. Stern: Buildings and Projects, 1987–1992, with an introduction by Vincent Scully (New York: Rizzoli, 1992), 196–97.

"Kiawah Island Beach Club" *Builder*, October 1996, 124.

Robert A. M. Stern: Buildings (New York: The Monacelli Press, 1996), 224–43.

Greenbrier at West Village Golf Resort
Fukushima Prefecture, Japan, 1990–1995

Associate Partner: Grant Marani. Project Associate: Joseph Andriola. Assistants: Todd Fauser, Adonica L. Inzer, Nancy K. Jordan, Lynn H. Wang, Rosamund Young. Associate Architect: MHS Planners, Architects & Engineers.

Clare Melhuish, "Present Tense," *Building Design*, May 17, 1991, 20–21.

Robert A. M. Stern: Buildings and Projects, 1987–1992, with an introduction by Vincent Scully (New York: Rizzoli, 1992), 314–15.

Nina Rappaport, "Exporting Architecture: New York Architects Abroad," *Oculus*, October 1995, 10–14.

Robert A. M. Stern: Buildings (New York: The Monacelli Press, 1996), 208–23.

"The Greenbrier West Village," *Shinkenchiku*, 1997, 240–46.

Residence in the Midwestern United States
1990–1992

Partner: Roger H. Seifter. Project Associate: John Berson. Assistants: Gary Brewer, Abigail M. Huffman, Daniel Romualdez, Diane Smith, Elizabeth A. Valella, Rosamund Young. Interiors Associate: Raúl Morillas. Interiors Assistants: Paul McDonnell, Witten Singer. Landscape Associates: Robert Ermerins, Charlotte M. Frieze.

Robert A. M. Stern: Buildings and Projects, 1987–1992, with an introduction by Vincent Scully (New York: Rizzoli, 1992), 318–19.

Robert A. M. Stern: Houses (New York: The Monacelli Press, 1997), 506–25.

Brooklyn Law School
Brooklyn, New York, 1990–1994

Project Architects: Paul Whalen, Partner; Barry Rice, Associate Partner.

392   Project Associate: Michael Jones. Project Assistants: Ferenc Annus, Victoria Delgado, Pablo Doval, Robert Han, Peter Himmelstein, Valerie Hughes, Warren James. Landscape Associate: Brian Sawyer. Landscape Assistant: Allison Towne. Associate Architect: Wank Adams Slavin Associates.

"Brooklyn Law School to Erect a $25M, 10-Story Addition," *New York Construction News*, February 25, 1991, 1, 5.

Clare Melhuish, "Present Tense," *Building Design*, May 17, 1991, 20–21.

Henrik Krogius, "Brooklyn Law Is Set to Add New Building," *Brooklyn Heights Press and Cobble Hill News*, February 27, 1992, 1, 13.

Robert A. M. Stern: Buildings and Projects, 1987–1992, with an introduction by Vincent Scully (New York: Rizzoli, 1992), 290–93.

Herbert Muschamp, "If You Squint, This Is Not a Faulty Tower," *New York Times*, August 21, 1994, H:32.

"Brooklyn Law School Tower," *AIA Annals*, 1994, 22.

"It's Official . . . Building is Formally Dedicated,"*Brooklyn Law School News*, spring 1995.

"Brooklyn Law School Tower, Brooklyn New York," *Classicist* 1:38.

Robert A. M. Stern: Buildings (New York: The Monacelli Press, 1996), 378–95.

Gabriele Tagliaventi, ed., *Rinascimento Urbano (Urban Renaissance)* (Bologna: Grafis Edizioni, 1996), 212–13.

Celebration
Celebration, Florida, 1987–1997

Partner: Paul Whalen. Project Associate: Daniel Lobitz. Assistants: Gary Brewer, Geoffrey Mouen, John Saunders, Tim Slattery, Derrick Smith. Co–Master Planner: Cooper, Robertson & Partners. Architect of Record: HKS, Inc.

Robert A. M. Stern: Buildings and Projects, 1987–1992, with an introduction by Vincent Scully (New York: Rizzoli, 1992), 344.

Christina Binkley, "Disney Finally Releases Plans for Village," *Wall Street Journal*, June 14, 1995, F:1, 4.

Shari Mycek, "A Clean Slate: Disney's Celebration of a Healthy Community," *Trustee*, September 1995, 6–10.

"Dance to Disney's Music," *Progressive Architecture*, October 1995, 19.

June Fletcher, "Dream-Builder Disney Offers Dream Homes," *Wall Street Journal*, October 20, 1995.

Carol Lawson, "When You Wish upon a House," *New York Times*, November 16, 1995, C:1, 6.

John Rothchild, "A Mouse in the House," *Time*, December 4, 1995, 62–63.

Ruth Eckdish Knack, "Once Upon a Town," *Planning* (American Planning Association), March 1996, 10–13.

Herbert Muschamp, "Can New Urbanism Find Room for the Old?," *New York Times*, June 2, 1996, 27.

Benjamin Woolley, "Disney's World," *Sunday Telegraph Magazine*, June 2, 1996, 16–19.

Boyce Thompson, "Two Worlds," *Builder*, July 1996, 21–22.

James D. Carper, "What Is Disney Celebrating?"; John Henry, "Is Celebration Mayberry or a Stepford Village?"; and Barry Berkus, "Disney Forgot People Will Live Here," *Professional Builder*, September 1996, 46–50.

Mary Doyle-Kimball, "Sizing Up Disney's Celebration," *Builder*, September 1996, 118–22.

Mary Shanklin, "Celebration of Architecture," *Orlando Sentinel*, September 22, 1996, F:6–7.

Emilio Tadini, "Mouston, Disneyworld," *Il Corriere della Sera*, September 23, 1996; reprinted in *Rassegna*, 1997, 2:58–59.

Michael Pollan, "Sticks & Stones: Mickey for Mayor?," *House & Garden*, October 1996, 61–72.

Russ Rymer, "Back to the Future: Disney Reinvents the Company Town," *Harper's Magazine*, October 1996, 65–71, 75–78.

Deborah Dietsch,"Disney Turns 25, Builds New Town," *Architecture*, November 1996, 38–39.

Dietmar Steiner, "A Diary of Disney's Celebration," *Domus*, November 1996, 43–52.

Carol Lawson, "Disney's Newest Show Is a Town," *New York Times*, November 16, 1996, B:1, 6.

Roger K. Lewis, "Disney's Old-Time Small Town Strains Under Weight of Big-Name Architects," *Washington Post*, December 14, 1996, E:5.

Beth Dunlop, *Building a Dream: The Art of Disney Architecture* (New York: Harry N. Abrams, 1996), 10–11, 193.

Gabriele Tagliaventi, ed., *Rinascimento Urbano (Urban Renaissance)* (Bologna: Grafis Edizioni, 1996), 170–71.

John Beardsley, "A Mickey Mouse Utopia," *Landscape Architecture*, February 1997, 76–83, 92–93.

D. Scott Middleton, "Celebration, Florida: Breaking New Ground," *Urban Land*, February 1997, 32–36, 54.

Robert Campbell, "Celebrating Community: Disney's Florida Development Is a Traditional Town," *Boston Globe*, February 2, 1997, N:1–2.

Seth Schiesel, "New Disney Vision Making the Future a Thing of the Past," *New York Times*, February 23, 1997, 1, 24.

Philip Morris, "Celebration," *Southern Accents*, March–April 1997, 98–100.

Marisa Bartolucci, "Architecture and the Corporate Landscape," *Metropolis*, June 1997, 56–59, 90–92.

Ann Carrns, "Architects Attack Development Style," *Wall Street Journal*, June 11, 1997, B:12.

Beth Dunlop, "Our Town, U.S.A.," *Disney Magazine*, summer 1997, 62–67.

Rick Edmonds, "The New Urbanism: Community as Amenity: Celebration," *Forum (Magazine of the Florida Humanities Council)*, summer 1997, 10–16.

Reed Kroloff, "Disney Builds a Town," *Architecture*, August 1997, 114–19.

Lynn Nesmith, "The Power of Place," *Southern Living*, September 1997, 92–99.

William L. Nolan, "The New American Neighborhood," *Better Homes and Gardens*, September 1997, 42ff.

Caroline E. Mayer, "The Mickey House Club," *Washington Post*, November 15, 1997, A:1, 22–23.

Michael Pollan, "Disney Discovers Real Life," *New York Times Magazine*, December 14, 1997, 56–63, 76–81, 88.

James Steele, *Architecture Today* (London: Phaidon Press, 1997), 360.

Carter Wiseman, *Shaping a Nation* (New York: W. W. Norton & Company, 1998), 380–81.

Residence in Starwood
Aspen, Colorado, 1991–1996

Associate Partner: Armand LeGardeur. Project Associate: Augusta Barone. Assistants: Adam Anuszkiewicz, Victoria Delgado, Luis Rueda-Salazar. Interiors Associate: Raúl Morillas. Interiors Assistant:

Christopher Powell. Landscape Associate: Brian Sawyer.

Robert A. M. Stern: Buildings and Projects, 1987–1992, with an introduction by Vincent Scully (New York: Rizzoli, 1992), 351.

Robert A. M. Stern: Houses (New York: The Monacelli Press, 1997), 280–315.

Feature Animation Building, The Walt Disney Company
Burbank, California, 1991–1994

Core and Shell: Project Architects: Paul Whalen, Partner; Barry Rice, Associate Partner. Project Associates: Michael Jones, Daniel Lobitz, Geoffrey Mouen. Assistant: Rosamund Young. Associate Architect: Morris Architects. Interior Architecture: Associate Partners: Alexander P. Lamis, Barry Rice. Assistants: Adam Anuszkiewicz, Valerie Hughes, Jane Whitford. Interiors Assistant: Pat Burns Ross. Associate Interiors Architect: Morris Architects.

Larry Gordon, "Back to the Drawing Board," *Los Angeles Times*, November 25, 1994, B:1, 3.

Aaron Betsky, "Cartoon Character," *Los Angeles Times Magazine*, December 18, 1994, 46–47.

"Disney's Fun Factory: Surreal Animation Building Roars to Life," *USA Today*, January 4, 1995, D:1.

Aaron Betsky, "Animated Architecture," *Architectural Record*, March 1995, 72–81.

Herbert Muschamp, "Playful, Even Goofy, but What Else? It's Disney," *New York Times*, March 5, 1995, 2:34.

Michael Webb, "Disney Animation," *Interiors*, May 1995, 46–53.

"Robert A. M. Stern: Feature Animation Building," *A+U (Architecture and Urbanism)*, August 1995, 16–27.

Dwight Young, "Frisky Buildings," *Preservation*, September–October 1996, 144.

Delia Sala, "Walt Disney Pictures' Feature Animation Studios," *Habitat Ufficio*, October–November 1996, 52–57.

"Feature Animation Building at Burbank, California," *Domus*, November 1996, 30–34.

Beth Dunlop, *Building a Dream: The Art of Disney Architecture* (New York: Harry N. Abrams, 1996), 17, 80, 170–71, 174–79.

Robert A. M. Stern: Buildings (New York: The Monacelli Press, 1996), 100–119.

James Steele, *Architecture Today* (London: Phaidon Press, 1997), 355, 360.

Colgate Darden School of Business, University of Virginia
Charlottesville, Virginia, 1992–1996

Partner: Graham S. Wyatt. Project Associate: Gary L. Brewer. Assistants: Joseph Andriola, Adam Anuszkiewicz, Augusta Barone, John Gilmer, Michael Granville, Adonica L. Inzer, Victor Jones, Alexander P. Lamis, Rosamund Young. Interiors Assistant: Pat Burns Ross. Landscape Associate: Robert Ermerins. Landscape Assistants: Charlotte M. Frieze, Sarah Newbery, Brian Sawyer. Associate Architect: Ayers/Saint/Gross Inc.

"Details," *Architecture*, April 1992, 24.

Robert A. M. Stern: Buildings and Projects, 1987–1992, with an introduction by Vincent Scully (New York: Rizzoli, 1992), 338–39.

Hawes C. Spencer, "New Darden," *Cville Weekly*, January 23–29, 1996, 8, 10.

"On Mr. Jefferson's Shoulders," *UVA Alumni Magazine*, April 1996, 5.

M. Lindsay Bierman, "A View of the Process: New Classicism in the Old Dominion," *Classicist* 3:56–63.

John Beardsley, "Doing Jefferson Wrong," *Landscape Architecture*, July 1996, 135, 136.

Karen Stein, "Business School Connects to Distant Past," *Architectural Record*, July 1996, 72–79.

Robert A. M. Stern: Buildings (New York: The Monacelli Press, 1996), 456–93.

David Maurer, "A New Take on Classicism at the University of Virginia," *Colonial Homes*, September 1997, 76–79.

Johann Matthaus von Mauch and Charles Pierre Joseph Normand, *Parallel of the Classical Orders of Architecture*, ed. Donald M. Rattner (New York: Acanthus Press, 1998), plates 5–7.

Red Oaks
Cohasset, Massachusetts, 1992–1996

Associate Partner: Randy M. Correll. Senior Assistant: Elizabeth Kozarec. Assistants: Victoria Delgado, Mike Jacobs. Landscape Associate: Robert Ermerins.

Robert A. M. Stern: Houses (New York: The Monacelli Press, 1997), 230–49.

Nanki-Shirahama Golf Clubhouse
Wakayama Prefecture, Japan, 1992

Associate Partner: Grant Marani. Assistants: Adam Anuszkiewicz, Lee Ledbetter, Derrick Smith.

Gap Embarcadero Building
San Francisco, California, 1992–2000

Partner: Graham S. Wyatt. Senior Assistants: Edwin Hofmann, Michael Jones, Lee Ledbetter. Assistants: Geoffrey Mouen, Antonio Ng, Anthony Polito, Michael Wilbur. Associate Architect: Gensler.

Gerald D. Adams, "N.Y. Architect Firm Gets the Gap Plum," *San Francisco Examiner*, December 2, 1992, C:1, 5.

"Business Briefs: Gap Picks Designer for Headquarters," *San Francisco Chronicle*, December 2, 1992, C:2.

"Details," *Architecture*, January 1993, 22.

"Details," *Architecture*, November 1994, 29.

Dan Levy, "GAP Wins OK for Site at SF Embarcadero," *San Francisco Chronicle*, January 11, 1995, A:20.

John King, "Filling an Architectural Gap," *San Francisco Chronicle*, January 20, 1997, B:1–4.

Residence
Kings Point, New York, 1992–1997

Partner: Roger H. Seifter. Project Associate: John Berson. Senior Assistant: Robert Epley. Assistants: Charles Brainerd, Jason DePierre, Amy Farber, Michael Levendusky, Robert Miller. Interiors Assistant: Peter Fleming. Landscape Associate: Charlotte M. Frieze. Landscape Assistant: Laura Hynes.

Aspen Highlands
Aspen, Colorado, 1992–2001

Partner: Graham S. Wyatt. Project Associate: Geoffrey Mouen. Project Architects: Joseph Andriola, Lee Ledbetter. Assistants: Jamie L. Alexander, Adam Anuszkiewicz, Augusta Barone, Sarah Bayliss, Tia Blassingame, Charles C. Brainerd, Barbara Austin Brown, Andrew Cottrill, John Gilmer, Susan Girvel, Grace Hinton, Bret Horton, Timothy Howell, Michael Jacobs, Victor Jones, Haven Knight, Rebecca Laubach, Breen Mahony, Grant Marani, Andrew McFarland, Katherine Oudens, Dennis Sagiev, John Saunders, Diane Scott, Carolyn Straub,

394   Javier Von Der Pahlen, Michael Wilbur, Paul Zamek, Paul Zembsch. Project Landscape Associates: Robert Ermerins, Brian Sawyer, Ann Stokes. Landscape Assistants: Janelle Denler, Mary Estes, Charlotte M. Frieze, Hannah Fusco, Alessandra Galletti, Gerrit Goss, Laura Hynes, Sarah Newbery, Allison Towne. Associate Architect: Cottle Graybeal Yaw Architects. Associate Architect: Kendall/Heaton Associates, Inc.

Scott Condon, "Hines Unveils his Plans for Highlands," *Aspen Times Daily*, June 16, 1993, 1, 13.

Dave Reed, "Hines Unwraps a New Highlands," *Aspen Daily News*, June 16, 1993, 1, 9.

Erin Perry, "Highlands Development a Done Deal," *Aspen Daily News*, October 30, 1997, 1, 4.

William Gates Computer Science Building, Stanford University
Palo Alto, California, 1992–1996

Project Architects: Graham S. Wyatt, Partner; Alexander P. Lamis, Associate Partner. Senior Assistant: Adam Anuszkiewicz. Assistants: Preston Gumberich, Victor Jones, Pat Burns Ross. Associate Architect: Fong & Chang Architects.

Alan Hess, "Stanford on the Outside, High-Tech on the Inside," *San Jose Mercury News*, February 25, 1996, C:1.

Aaron Betsky, "Stanford Recaptures Lost Grandeur," *Architectural Record*, July 1996, 66–71.

Michael Cannell, "Recapturing the Pride of Place," *Stanford Today*, September–October 1996, 48–55.

Robert A. M. Stern: Buildings (New York: The Monacelli Press, 1996), 434–55.

NEAR WEST CAMPUS
Palo Alto, California, 1994

Project Architects: Graham S. Wyatt, Partner; Alexander P. Lamis, Associate Partner. Assistants: Adam Anuszkiewicz, Lynn Wang, Youngmin Woo, Paul Zamek.

Residence at Skimhampton
East Hampton, New York, 1992–1993

Associate Partner: Randy M. Correll. Senior Assistant: Daniel Romualdez.

Paul Goldberger, "Robert A. M. Stern Takes on the Critic's Modernist Box," *Architectural Digest*, February 1995, 28, 30, 34, 37, 40–41.

Robert A. M. Stern: Houses (New York: The Monacelli Press, 1997), 440–49.

Residence
Telluride, Colorado, 1992

Associate Partner: Armand LeGardeur. Assistant: Elizabeth Kozarec.

Residence in Beverly Park
Beverly Hills, California, 1993–1994

Associate Partner: Arthur Chabon. Senior Assistant: Rosamund Young. Assistants: Victoria Delgado, Victor Jones, Roxana Klein. Landscape Associate: Robert Ermerins. Landscape Assistants: Charlotte M. Frieze, Brian Sawyer.

Additions to Points of View
Seal Harbor, Maine, 1992–1993

Associate Partner: Armand LeGardeur. Assistants: Victoria Delgado, Elizabeth Kozarec, Lee Ledbetter.

Steven M. L. Aronson, "Maine Prospects: Energetic Additions for a Shingle Style House," *Architectural Digest*, June 1996, 163–67, 202.

Robert A. M. Stern: Houses (New York: The Monacelli Press, 1997), 70–87.

42nd Street Now!
New York, New York, 1992–2001

Partner: Paul Whalen. Senior Assistant: Grace Hinton. Assistants: Charles Brainerd, Lee Ledbetter, John Libertino, Daniel Lobitz, Andrew McFarland, Molly Mikula, Julie Nelson, John Saunders, Tim Slattery. Graphics and Signage Design: M&Co. Retail Architect: Haverson Rockwell Architects. Lighting Design: Fisher Marantz Renfro Stone.

David W. Dunlap, "New Times Sq. Plan: Lights! Signs! Dancing! Hold the Offices," *New York Times*, August 20, 1992, B:3.

Herbert Muschamp, "Architecture View: The Alchemy Needed to Rethink Times Square," *New York Times*, August 30, 1992, 2:24.

"Briefs: Projects," *Architectural Record*, October 1992, 28.

"News Report," *Progressive Architecture*, October 1992, 22.

Peter Slatin, "New Plans for New York," *Architecture*, October 1992, 25.

Herbert Muschamp, "Time to Reset the Clock in Times Square," *New York Times*, November 1, 1992, 2:1, 28.

David W. Dunlap, "Rethinking 42nd St. for Next Decade," *New York Times*, June 27, 1993, 10:1, 4.

Amie Wallach, "Sizzling on 42nd Street," *New York Newsday*, July 8, 1993, 54–55.

Herbert Muschamp, "42nd Street Plan: Be Bold or Begone!," *New York Times*, September 19, 1993, H:33.

Kurt Anderson, "Spectator: Can 42nd Street Be Born Again?," *Time*, September 27, 1993, 93.

Peter Slatin, "Forty-Second Street Part I: What You Might Still Want to Know about 42nd Street," *Oculus*, November 1993, 10, 11.

Peter Slatin, "Forty-Second Street Part II: The Scenario Unfolds," *Oculus*, December 1993, 10–12.

"Times Square on the Mind," *Planning*, October 1994, 26.

Donald Martin Reynolds, *The Architecture of New York City* (New York: John Wiley & Sons, 1994), 207–8.

Herbert Muschamp, "A Flare For Fantasy: 'Miami Vice' Meets 42nd Street," *New York Times*, May 21, 1995, 2:1, 27.

Bradford McKee, "Times Square Revival," *Architecture*, November 1995, 94–99.

Deborah K. Dietsch, "Disney's New Urban Influence," *Architecture*, December 1995, 15.

New York: The World's Premier Public Theater, with an essay by Robert A. M. Stern and Thomas Mellins (New York: Columbia Books of Architecture, Columbia University, 1995), 31–33.

Kira Gould, "Times Square: On Its Way Back . . . But As What?," *Oculus*, February 1996, 8.

Charles K. Hoyt, "Times Square Victory," *Architectural Record*, February 1996, 66–71.

Randall Mason, "Design as a Political Process," *Metropolis*, April 1996, 97, 99, 101.

Frank Rose, "Can Disney Tame 42nd Street?," *Fortune*, June 24, 1996, 94–104.

Paul Goldberger, "The New Times Square: Magic that Surprised the Magicians," *New York Times*, October 15, 1996, C:11–12.

Paul Goldberger, "An Old Jewel of 42nd St. Reopens, Seeking to Dazzle Families," *New York Times*, December 11, 1996, 1.

Ada Louise Huxtable, "Architecture: Miracle on 42nd Street," *Wall*

Street Journal, April 3, 1997, A:16.

Bruce Handy, "Miracle on 42nd Street," *Time*, April 7, 1997, 68–70, 72.

Herbert Muschamp, "A Palace for a New Magic Kingdom, 42nd Street," *New York Times*, May 11, 1997, 2:1, 39.

Allen Freeman and Martin Bloom. "The Show Goes On: As Times Square's Lights Burn Brighter, 42nd Street Rises From the Dead," *Preservation*, May–June 1997, 72–79.

Rick Lyman, "As the Great White Way Turns a Corner," *New York Times*, May 8, 1998, E:1, 8.

East Hampton Library
East Hampton, New York, 1992–1997

Associate Partner: Randy M. Correll. Project Associate: Preston Gumberich. Assistants: Jamie Alexander, John Saunders. Interiors Assistant: Christopher Powell.

Kelly Ann Smith, "East Hampton Library at 100," *New York Times*, September 28, 1997, 22.

"Facilities Showcase: New Construction . . . and Renovation," *American Libraries*, April 1998, 71.

Hotel Melayu
Kuala Lumpur, Malaysia, 1992

Partner: Paul Whalen. Senior Assistants: Joseph Andriola, Daniel Lobitz. Assistants: Roxana Klein, Geoffrey Mouen, John Saunders, Brian Sawyer, Ralf Sturzebecher.

Moore Psychology Building, Dartmouth College
Hanover, New Hampshire, 1992–1999

Partner: Graham S. Wyatt. Project Associate: Preston Gumberich. Assistants: Elizabeth Adams, Augusta Barone, Ricardo Alvarez-Diaz, Jonas Goldberg, Adonica Inzer, Claudia Lin, Meghan McDermott, Andre Mellone, Richard Schneider. Interiors Associate: Pat Burns Ross. Interiors Assistant: Claire Ratliff.

"New Psych Building Due in '99," *Dartmouth Life*, June 1997, 1–2.

Disney's BoardWalk
Walt Disney World, Lake Buena Vista, Florida, 1993–1996

Partner: Paul Whalen. Project Associate: John Gilmer. Assistants: Gary Brewer, Michael Jones, Daniel Lobitz, Geoffrey Mouen, John Saunders, Jayne Whitford, Paul Zamek. Landscape Associate: Robert Ermerins. Landscape Assistants: Charlotte M. Frieze, Laura Schoenbaum. Associate Architect: HKS, Inc.

Robert A. M. Stern: Buildings and Projects, 1987–1992, with an introduction by Vincent Scully (New York: Rizzoli, 1992), 350.

Matteo Vercelloni, "Heterotopias of Compensation: Disney Theme Parks and Their Hotel Structures," *Domus*, November 1996, 35–42.

Joe Sharkey, "Boardwalk of Make-Believe," *New York Times*, December 9, 1996, B:1, 2.

Beth Dunlop, *Building a Dream: The Art of Disney Architecture* (New York: Harry N. Abrams, 1996), 80, 189.

Mel Allen, "Walking the Boards," *Disney Magazine*, spring 1997, 36–37, 40.

John P. Radulski, "Disney's BoardWalk," *Hospitality Design*, September–October 1997, 67–73.

Residence in Preston Hollow
Dallas, Texas, 1993–1999

Associate Partner: Armand LeGardeur. Assistants: Diane Boston, Victoria Delgado, Luis Rueda-Salazar, Doug Wright, Susi Yu. Interiors Associate: Raúl Morillas. Interiors Assistants: Peter Fleming, Christopher

Powell, Cynthia Smith. Landscape Associate: Brian Sawyer. Landscape Assistants: Allison Towne, Laura Hynes, Sarah Newbery, Ahmad-ali Sarder-Afkhami.

Concert Hall and Museum
Karuizawa, Japan, 1993

Associate Partner: Grant Marani. Assistants: Michael Jones, Luis Rueda-Salazar.

Celebration Health
Celebration, Florida, 1993–1998

Partner: Paul Whalen. Project Associate: Michael Jones. Assistants: Ferenc Annus, Marina Annus, John Saunders, Michael Wilbur, Jennifer Wlock. Interiors Assistant: Christopher Powell. Landscape Associate: Brian Sawyer. Associate Architect: NBBJ.

Patricia B. Limbacher, "Disney's Dream," *Modern Healthcare*, October 20, 1997, 30–33.

Product Design
HBF
Partner: Paul Whalen. Assistants: John Gilmer, Daniel Lobitz, Dennis Sagiev.

BALDINGER
Partner: Paul Whalen. Project Associate: William Georgis. Assistant: Daniel Lobitz.

SASAKI
Partner: Paul Whalen. Assistants: John Ellis, John Gilmer.

Devon Jarvis, "Cutting Edge," *In Style*, July 1997, 165.

Residence
Montecito, California, 1993–1998

Partner: Roger H. Seifter. Project Associate: John Berson. Assistants: Monique Agnew, Jamie Alexander, Joseph Andriola, Joel Barkley, Amy Farber, Anselm Fusco, Michael Jacobs, Victor Jones, Lisa Shire. Landscape Associates: Robert Ermerins, Charlotte M. Frieze, Brian Sawyer, Ann Stokes. Landscape Assistants: Laura Hynes, Allison Towne.

Residence at North York
Toronto, Ontario, Canada, 1993–1998

Partner: Roger H. Seifter. Project Associate: Daniel Lobitz. Assistants: Monique Agnew, John Gilmer, Michael Levendusky, Renan Pierre. Landscape Associate: Brian Sawyer. Landscape Assistant: Sarah Newbery. Associate Architect: R. H. Carter Architects.

The American Houses of Robert A. M. Stern, with an introduction by Clive Aslet (New York: Rizzoli, 1991), 216–19.

Robert A. M. Stern: Buildings and Projects, 1987–1992, with an introduction by Vincent Scully (New York: Rizzoli, 1992), 310–11.

Smith Campus Center, Pomona College
Claremont, California, 1993–1999

Partner: Graham S. Wyatt. Project Associates: Adam Anuszkiewicz, Diane Scott. Assistants: Kyo Bannai, John Cays, Preston Gumberich, Rebecca Laubach, Tonia Long, Lenore Passavanti. Interiors Associate: Raúl Morillas. Interiors Senior Assistant: Cynthia Smith. Landscape Associate: Brian Sawyer. Landscape Assistant: Allison Towne.

National Advocacy Center, U.S. Department of Justice, University of South Carolina
Columbia, South Carolina, 1993–1998

Partner: Graham S. Wyatt. Project Associate: Gary Brewer. Senior Assistant: Diane Scott. Assistant: Tim Howell. Interiors Associate: Pat Burns Ross. Landscape Associate: Ann Stokes. Associate Architects:

396   HNTB, Watson-Tate Architects.

Ann C. Sullivan, "Improving EIFS Performance," *Architecture*, May 1996, 251–53.

Clif LeBlanc, "Reno Wants Center to Fight Digital Crime," *The State* (Columbia, South Carolina), June 2, 1998, A:1, 6.

Life Dream House
1994

Project Associate: Gary Brewer. Assistants: Joel Barkley, Robert Epley, Tim Slattery.

Stephen Petranek and Jennifer Allen, "A House for All America," *Life*, June 1994, 82–92.

"Stern Bats 500," *Architectural Record*, January 1995, 15.

Kenneth Miller, "Last Year's Dream House: Raising the Roof," *Life*, June 1995, 93–98.

Kenneth Miller, "Dream House '94: Robert A. M. Stern's Creation Turns Up in a New Community Modeled on the Best of the Past," *Life*, May 1996.

Amy Greene, "Elegant Show House Makes Style and Space Affordable," *Atlanta Journal-Constitution*, June 7, 1996, D:1.

Kathy Greet, "Stern's Eye View," *Builder*, December 1996, 76–77.

Tracie Rohzon, "The House Is in the Mail," *New York Times*, July 2, 1998, F:1.

Temple Emanu-el
Closter, New Jersey, 1994–

Associate Partner: Alexander P. Lamis. Assistants: Michael Jones, Grant Marani, Andre Mellone, Lynn Wang, Youngmin Woo. Landscape Associate: Brian Sawyer.

Math/Science Building and Library, Taft School
Watertown, Connecticut, 1994

Partner: Graham S. Wyatt. Senior Assistant: Adam Anuszkiewicz. Assistants: Joel Barkley, Janelle Denler, Rowena Evans, Roxana Klein, Steven Roberts, Carolyn Straub, Jeffrey Tucker, Youngmin Woo, Paul Zamek.

Porto Sauipe Marina Village
Bahia, Salvador, Brazil, 1994

Partner: Paul Whalen. Senior Assistant: Joseph Andriola. Assistant: Andre Mellone. Local Architect: André Sá.

Pacific Heights Residence
San Francisco, California, 1994–1998

Associate Partner: Grant Marani. Senior Assistants: Elizabeth Kozarec, Katherine Oudens. Assistants: Johnny Cruz, Andre Mellone.

U.S. Courthouse and IRS Complex
Beckley, West Virginia, 1994–1999

Associate Partner: Grant Marani. Project Associate: Elizabeth Kozarec. Assistants: John Gilmer, Dino Marcantonio. Interiors Assistant: Scott Sloat. Landscape Design: Sarah Newbery. Associate Architect: Einhorn Yaffee Prescott.

Bradford McKee, "On the Boards: U.S. Courthouse and Federal Complex, Beckley, West Virginia," *Architecture*, November 1994, 41.

Michael Wise, "Courthouses on Trial," *Metropolis*, May 1995, 100.

Edward Gunts, "Federal Courthouse Competition," *Architecture*, January 1996, 105–9.

600 Thirteenth Street, N.W.
Washington, D.C., 1994–1997

Associate Partner: Barry Rice. Project Associates: Joseph Andriola, Lynn Wang. Senior Assistant: Edwin Hofmann. Assistant: Tim Howell. Landscape Architect: Charlotte M. Frieze. Associate Architects: Kendall/Heaton Associates, Shalom Baranes Associates.

Bradford McKee, "Washington's Planning Politics," *Architecture*, November 1997, 47–53.

Benjamin Forgey, "Cityscape: Short and Sweet: Architect Robert A. M. Stern Rises to D.C.'s Height Limit," *Washington Post*, January 3, 1998, G:1, 7–8.

Roger K. Lewis, "Shaping the City: A Mismatch of Designs on 13th Street NW," *Washington Post*, January 10, 1998, E:1, 6.

Residence in Southampton
Southampton, New York, 1994–1997

Associate Partner: Randy M. Correll. Project Associate: Geoffrey Mouen. Assistant: Tim Slattery. Landscape Associate: Charlotte M. Frieze. Landscape Assistant: Laura Hynes.

Prototypical Stores for eighteen 77
Short Hills, New Jersey; King of Prussia, Pennsylvania; Woodfield Center, Illinois, 1994–1996

Partner: Graham S. Wyatt. Project Associate: Joseph Andriola. Senior Assistant: Paul Kariouk. Assistants: Krystyan Keck, Paul Zamek. Associate Architect: Kubala, Washatko Architects, Inc.

Robert A. M. Stern: Buildings (New York: The Monacelli Press, 1996), 256–63.

Saigon Metropolitan Tower
Ho Chi Minh City (Saigon), Vietnam, 1994

Partner: Paul Whalen. Senior Assistant: Adam Anuszkiewicz. Assistant: Carolyn Straub.

Navesink Residence
Middletown, New Jersey, 1994–1999

Associate Partner: Arthur Chabon. Project Associate: Augusta Barone. Assistants: Victoria Delgado, Angela Dirks, Andre Mellone, Lenore Passavanti, Pamela Trevithick, Jennifer Wlock. Landscape Associate: Charlotte M. Frieze. Landscape Assistant: Daisy Reeves.

Residence Hall for Columbia University
New York, New York, 1996–2000

Associate Partner: Alexander P. Lamis. Senior Assistant: Christine Kelley. Assistants: John Ellis, Kevin Galvin, Alex Karmeinsky, Ed Leveckis, Tonia Long, Howard Shen, Tom VanDeWeghe, Youngmin Woo.

Janet Allon, "A Storm over a Dorm Plan," *New York Times*, March 17, 1996, 13:8.

Toby Axelrod, "Columbia's Deconstructionists," *New York Observer*, May 13, 1996, 10.

Hans Chen, "New Dorm Architect Proposes Plan to Area Residents," *Columbia Spectator*, March 25, 1997, 1, 5.

"A New Den for the Lions of Columbia," *New York Times*, April 20, 1997, 9:1.

David Garrard Lowe, "Urbanities: Now They're Deconstructing the Columbia Campus," *City Journal*, Autumn 1997, 84–97.

Barry Bergdoll, *Mastering McKim's Plan: Columbia's First Century on Morningside Heights* (New York: Miriam and Ira D. Wallach Art Gallery, Columbia University in the City of New York, 1997), 241–42.

Benjamin Lowe, "$50 Million Dorm Stirs Talk," *Columbia Spectator,* February 11, 1998, 1, 5.

Janet Allon, "Dormitory Plan: One Minus, Many Pluses," *New York Times,* February 22, 1998, 6.

Erik Seadale, "Town and Gown Marry on Columbia Dorm Plan," *New York Observer,* March 9, 1998, 10.

Residence and Guest House at Katama
Martha's Vineyard, Massachusetts, 1995–1997

Associate Partner: Randy M. Correll. Assistants: Geoffrey Mouen, Naomi Neville, Kathy Pacchiana, Tim Slattery. Landscape Associate: Charlotte M. Frieze.

Stephen A. Kliment, "Island Themes Revisited: Expanding the Shingle Style Tradition on Martha's Vineyard," *Architectural Digest,* July 1998, 90–95.

U.S. Department of State Office Building Chancery
Berlin, Germany, 1995

Partner: Graham S. Wyatt. Project Associates: Joseph Andriola, Preston Gumberich. Assistants: Peter Cornell, Adonica Inzer, Paul Kariouk, Michael Wilbur. Landscape Associate: Brian Sawyer. Landscape Assistant: Janell Denler. Associate Architect: Leo A. Daly.

James S. Russell, "Berlin's New U.S. Embassy: Safeguarding a Symbol," *Architectural Record,* March 1996, 36–43.

Reed Kroloff, "A New Embassy in Berlin," *Architecture,* April 1996, 131–36.

"Wettbewerb US-Botschaft am Pariser Platz Nr. 2 in Berlin," *Bauwelt,* July 5, 1996, 1464–70, 1498.

Sebastian Redecke and Ralph Stern, eds., *Foreign Affairs: Neue Botschaftsbauten und das Auswärtige Amt in Berlin (New Embassy Buildings and the German Foreign Office in Berlin)* (Berlin: Birkhäuser Verlag, 1997), 173, 192–95.

Newport Bay Club Convention Center
Paris Disneyland, France, 1995–1997

Associate Partner: Alexander P. Lamis. Senior Assistant: Tom VanDeWeghe. Assistants: David Solomon, Lynn Wang, Youngmin Woo. Interiors Assistant: Scott Sloat. Associate Architect: Oger International.

Georges Binder, "Immobilier international: Centres de congrès," *Bâtiment,* December 1996–January 1997, 10–11.

Master Plan and Addition to Knott Science Center, College of Notre Dame of Maryland
MASTER PLAN
Baltimore, Maryland, 1995–1997

Partner: Graham S. Wyatt. Project Associate: Augusta Barone. Assistant: Edwin Hofmann. Landscape Associate: Ann Stokes.

KNOTT SCIENCE CENTER
Baltimore, Maryland, 1997–

Partner: Graham S. Wyatt. Project Associate: Augusta Barone. Assistants: James Johnson, Dennis Sagiev. Landscape Associate: Ann Stokes. Associate Architect: George Vaeth Associates.

Bangor Public Library
Bangor, Maine, 1995–1998

Associate Partner: Alexander P. Lamis. Project Associates: Adam Anuszkiewicz, Elizabeth Kozarec. Senior Assistant: Tom VanDeWeghe. Assistants: Preston Gumberich, Tonia Long, Andre Mellone, Kim Neuscheler, David Solomon, Lynn Wang, Youngmin Woo. Interiors Assistants: Peter Fleming, Christopher Powell. Landscape Assistant: Sarah Newbery.

Tom Weber, "Library Unshelves Plans," *Bangor Daily News,* April 22–23, 1995, A:1, 6.

Jeff Clark, "Better than Ever," *Down East,* December 1997, 61–63.

Tom Weber, "The Return of the Bangor Library," *Bangor Daily News,* January 24–25, 1998, A:1, 6.

Alicia Anstead, "Bangor Public Library Reopens to Appreciative Public," *Bangor Daily News,* January 27, 1998, A:1, 10.

Seven Books in a Footlocker (Bangor: Bangor Public Library, 1998), 37–42; plates 28–31.

U.S. Courthouse Annex
Savannah, Georgia, 1995–

Associate Partner: Barry Rice. Project Associate: Joseph Andriola. Senior Assistant: Paul Zembsch. Assistants: Ricardo Alvarez-Diaz, Claudia Lin. Interiors Assistant: Scott Sloat. Landscape Associate: Charlotte M. Frieze. Landscape Assistant: Gerrit Goss.

Bradford McKee, "Federal Design Excellence," *Architecture,* January 1996, 60–95, 84.

John Cheves, "Savannahians Get to Speak Out on Federal Courthouse Annex," *Savannah News-Press,* February 22, 1996, A:1, 3.

Mary Bostwick Steinmetz, "The Proposed Federal Courthouse Annex in Savannah: A Rallying Point for Preservationists, Students, and Residents," *NCPE News (Newsletter of the National Council for Preservation Education),* June 1996, 1, 3–5.

Richard Fogaley, "Panel: Make Annex Design Changes," *Savannah Morning News,* October 21, 1997, C:1, 20.

Chuck Twardy, "East Coast USA: Living for the Moment," *World Architecture,* December 1997–January 1998, 88.

Michael Cannell, "Doing Justice," *Washington Post Magazine,* February 8, 1998, 18–22, 32, 34.

South Campus Housing, West Quadrangle, University of South Carolina
Columbia, South Carolina, 1995–1997

Partner: Graham S. Wyatt. Project Associate: Gary Brewer. Assistants: Adonica Inzer, Tonia Long, Michael Wilbur. Interiors Associate: Pat Burns Ross. Interiors Assistants: Peter Fleming, Fawn Galli. Landscape Associate: Ann Stokes. Associate Architect: Watson-Tate Architects, Inc.

Spring Valley Residence
Washington, D.C., 1995–

Associate Partner: Randy M. Correll. Senior Assistant: Naomi Neville. Assistants: Molly Denver, Shannon Gallagher, Tim Slattery.

Union Square South
New York, New York, 1995

Partner: Paul Whalen. Associate Partners: Alexander P. Lamis, Barry Rice. Project Associates: Adam Anuszkiewicz, Michael Jones. Assistants: Monique Agnew, Youngmin Woo.

Yawkey Park
Boston, Massachusetts, 1995

Project Architects: Graham S. Wyatt, Partner; Barry Rice, Associate Partner. Senior Assistant: John Gilmer. Assistant: Andre Mellone. Associate Architect: Devine deFlon Yaeger Architects.

Tribeca Park
Battery Park City, New York, New York, 1995–1999

Associate Partner: Barry Rice. Project Associate: Michael Jones. Senior Assistant: Christine Kelley. Interiors Assistant: Cynthia Smith. Associate

398   Architect: CK Architects.

Jayne Merkel, "Expanding Battery Park City," *Oculus*, June 1996, 11.

"Tax Abatements and Exemptions Help Manhattan's Battery Park City Rise Again," *Architectural Record*, August 1996, 48–49.

Edison Field
Anaheim, California, 1995–1998

Associate Partner: Barry Rice. Project Associate: John Gilmer. Senior Assistant: Howard Shen. Assistants: Kyo Bannai, Molly Denver, Kurt Glauber, Edwin Hofmann, Christine Kelley, Andre Mellone, Julie Nelson, Dan Parolek, Dennis Sagiev, David Solomon, Paul Zamek. Associate Architect: HOK Sport.

Marla Jo Fisher, "Architecture: Renovated Stadium Is a Product of Disney Whimsy and Baseball Tradition," *Orange County Register*, March 26, 1998., G:2.

Bill Shaikin, "One on One with Michael Eisner," *Los Angeles Times*, April 1, 1998, C:1, 7.

John W. Swanson, "A New Game in Town for Baseball Fans," *Anaheim Bulletin Weekly*, April 9, 1998, 14.

Roger Teffi, "Dream Team: How Architects, Designers, Imagineers Built Edison Field," *Orange County Business Journal*, April 13, 1998, 1, 17–18.

Miller Field
Milwaukee, Wisconsin, 1995

Partner: Graham S. Wyatt. Project Associate: John Gilmer. Assistants: Kyo Bannai, Kim Neuscheler, Pamela Trevithick. Landscape Assistant: Sarah Newbery.

"Stadium Design Weds Opposites," *Milwaukee Journal Sentinel*, December 3, 1995.

Residence on Kiawah Island
South Carolina, 1995–

Partner: Roger H. Seifter. Senior Assistant: Monique Agnew. Assistant: Victoria Baran. Landscape Associate: Ann Stokes.

Disney Ambassador Hotel
Urayasu-shi, Chiba-ken, Japan, 1996–

Partner: Paul Whalen. Project Associate: John Gilmer. Assistants: Hernan Chebar, Sharn Forster, Shannon Gallagher, Allison Karn, Liliana Lau, Rebecca Laubach, John Libertino, Andre Mellone, Kim Neuscheler, Tamie Noponen, David Solomon, Pamela Trevithick. Interiors Associate: Raúl Morillas. Interiors Assistants: Peter Fleming, Scott Sloat, Cynthia Smith. Landscape Associates: Brian Sawyer, Ann Stokes. Landscape Assistants: Alessandra Galletti, Karen Herskovitz. Associate Architect: Nikken Sekkei Ltd.

House at the Point
Santa Lucia Preserve, Monterey County, California, 1996

Associate Partner: Armand LeGardeur. Assistants: Diane Boston, Susi Yu.

National Storytelling Center
Jonesborough, Tennessee, 1996–

Project Associate: Gary Brewer. Assistants: Jori Erdman, Christine Kelley, Tonia Long, Katherine Oudens. Associate Architect: Ken Ross Architects, Inc. Landscape Architect: Andropogon. Interpretation: Ralph Appelbaum Associates, Inc.

Mulholland House
Los Angeles, California, 1996

Partner: Roger H. Seifter. Assistant: Michael Levendusky.

Wellesley Office Park
Wellesley, Massachusetts, 1996

Partner: Graham S. Wyatt. Senior Assistant: Joseph Andriola.

Residence
Greenwich, Connecticut, 1994

Associate Partner: Randy M. Correll. Assistants: Grace Hinton, Elizabeth Kozarec, Geoffrey Mouen, Tim Slattery. Interiors Associates: Raúl Morillas, Pat Burns Ross. Interiors Assistant: Claire Ratliff. Landscape Associate: Charlotte M. Frieze.

Residence
Denver, Colorado, 1996–

Associate Partner: Armand LeGardeur. Assistants: Susan Egan, Carmen Gonzalez, Andre Mellone, Doug Wright, Susi Yu. Interiors Associate: Raúl Morillas. Interiors Assistants: Peter Fleming, Scott Sloat. Landscape Associate: Brian Sawyer.

Federal Reserve Bank of Atlanta Headquarters
Atlanta, Georgia, 1996–

Partner: Graham S. Wyatt. Project Associate: Michael Jones. Assistants: Mai Jinn Chen, John Ellis, Shannon Gallagher, Kurt Glauber, Carey Jackson-Yonce, Victor Jones, Robert Lucas. Interiors Assistant: Peter Fleming. Landscape Assistant: Mary Estes, Sarah Newbery. Associate Architect: Smallwood, Reynolds, Stewart, Stewart & Associates, Inc.

Sallye Salter, "A New Face for the Fed," *Atlanta Journal & Constitution*, June 24, 1998, 1.

Catherine Fox, "Sense of Tradition Also Will Move to Midtown," *Atlanta Journal & Constitution*, June 25, 1998, G:2.

Sallye Salter, "Reserve Shows Off Plans for New Digs," *Atlanta Journal & Constitution*, June 25, 1998, G:2.

Maria Saporta, "Design Won't Strip Neighborhood Vision," *Atlanta Journal & Constitution*, June 25, 1998, G:2.

Catherine Fox, "Fed Secure in Its New Design," *Atlanta Journal & Constitution*, July 5, 1998, K:5.

Heavenly View Ranch
Old Snowmass, Colorado, 1996–1998

Associate Partner: Randy M. Correll. Senior Assistant: Diane Boston. Assistants: Monica Chiodo, Karina Teggeler. Interiors Associate: Pat Burns Ross. Interiors Assistant: Fawn Galli.

Diagonal Mar Entertainment and Retail Center
Barcelona, Spain, 1996–

Partner: Graham S. Wyatt. Assistants: Robert Lucas, Michael Wilbur. Associate Architects: Kendall Heaton Associates, Tusquets Diaz & Associates. Retail Architect: Communication Arts. Landscape Architect: EDAW.

Preservation and Development Plan
Heiligendamm, Germany, 1996–

Partner: Paul Whalen. Project Associate: Daniel Lobitz. Assistants: Kevin Galvin, Liliana Lau, Maggie Mahboubian, Andre Mellone, Tamie Noponen, Renan Pierre. Landscape Associate: Ann Stokes. Landscape Assistants: Alessandra Galletti, Sarah Newbery. Associate Architect: Kaiser Hohlbein.

Hobby Center for the Performing Arts
Houston, Texas, 1996–

Associate Partner: Barry Rice. Project Associate: Adam Anuszkiewicz.

Senior Assistant: Anselm Fusco. Assistants: John Cays, Hernan Chebar, John Esposito, Matthew Formicola, Gary Gonya, Rebecca Laubach, Tamie Noponen, Anthony Polito. Interiors Assistants: Peter Fleming, Scott Sloat.

New York Coliseum Site
New York, New York, 1996–1998

Associate Partner: Alexander P. Lamis. Assistants: John Ellis, Michael Flaherty, Anselm Fusco, Kurt Glauber, Michael Jones, Claudia Lin, Aanen Olsen, Howard Shen, Michael Wilson, Youngmin Woo. Associate Architect: CK Architects.

David Dunlap, "At Coliseum, Real Estate Lions Become Gladiators," *New York Times*, January 12, 1997, 9:7.

Ada Louise Huxtable, "Architecture: Feeding the Coliseum to the Lions," *Wall Street Journal*, January 14, 1997, A:18.

Herbert Muschamp, "Architecture View: Worthy of a World Capital," *New York Times*, January 19, 1997, 2:41.

Jayne Merkel, "Dissecting Columbus Circle," *Oculus*, May 1997, 14–16.

Devin Leonard, "The Little Old Ladies Prepare to Kill Again Over Columbus Circle," *New York Observer*, June 23, 1997, 1, 10.

Residence
Mount Kisco, New York, 1996

Associate Partner: Arthur Chabon. Project Associate: Augusta Barone. Assistants: Andre Mellone, Pamela Trevithick.

Guest House and Tennis Pavilion in Brentwood
Los Angeles, California, 1996–1998

Associate Partner: Randy M. Correll. Senior Assistant: Naomi Neville. Interiors Associate: Pat Burns Ross. Interiors Assistant: Fawn Galli. Landscape Associate: Charlotte M. Frieze. Landscape Assistant: Ashley Christopher.

Residence in Napa County
Oakville, California, 1996–

Partner: Roger H. Seifter. Senior Assistant: Robert Epley. Assistant: Elise Geiger. Landscape Associate: Ann Stokes. Landscape Assistant: Ashley Christopher.

Residence
Long Island, New York, 1997–

Partner: Roger H. Seifter. Project Associate: John Gilmer. Assistants: Ricardo Alvarez-Diaz, Catherine Popple, David Solomon. Landscape Associate: Charlotte M. Frieze. Landscape Assistant: Gerrit Goss.

Edgewater Apartments
West Vancouver, British Columbia, Canada, 1997–1999

Associate Partner: Barry Rice. Senior Assistant: Dennis Giobbe. Assistants: Matthew Formicola, Rashid Saxton, Howard Shen. Interiors Assistant: Scott Sloat. Landscape Associate: Charlotte M. Frieze. Landscape Assistant: Alessandra Galletti. Associate Architect: Lawrence Doyle Architect, Inc.

Belas Clube de Campo
Lisbon, Portugal, 1997–

Partner: Paul Whalen. Project Associate: Daniel Lobitz. Senior Assistant: Liliana Lau. Assistants: Mark Gage, Dennis Giobbe.

Welcome Center, Give Kids the World
Kissimmee, Florida, 1997–

Partner: Paul Whalen. Project Associate: John Gilmer. Assistants: Allison

Karn, Maggie Mahboubian. Associate Architect: HLM Design.

Tuxedo Reserve
Tuxedo, New York, 1997–

Partner: Paul Whalen. Project Associate: Daniel Lobitz. Senior Assistant: Jeffery Povero. Assistants: Mark Gage, Liliana Lau, Maggie Mahboubian, John Mueller.

Ian Koski, "Tuxedo at a Crossroads," *Southern Orange Record Weekly* (Middletown, New York), August 14, 1997, 1, 7.

Maharani Menari Tower
Jakarta, Indonesia, 1997

Partner: Paul Whalen. Senior Assistant: Michael Wilbur. Assistant: Edwin Hofmann.

Trump St. Moritz Condominiums
New York, New York, 1997

Project Associate: Michael Jones. Assistants: Shannon Gallagher, Kurt Glauber, Rob Lucas. Interiors Assistant: Cynthia Smith. Associate Architect: CK Architects.

"Stern Gets Trumped at the St. Moritz," *New York*, February 23, 1998, 18.

Tracie Rozhon, "Out with the Old, In with the Old-Fashioned," *New York Times*, April 20, 1998, B:1, 4.

Office Building and Parking Garage
Yonkers, New York, 1997–

Partner: Paul Whalen. Project Associate: Daniel Lobitz. Senior Assistant: Maggie Mahboubian. Assistants: Liliana Lau, Jeffery Povero.

Len Maniace, "Spencer Pledges Waterfront Complex 'Will Be Built,'" *Yonkers Herald-Statesman*, January 16, 1998, 3A.

Len Maniace, "Yonkers Hopes Noted Architect's Plan Boosts Waterfront," *Yonkers Herald-Statesman*, January 18, 1998, 3A.

Residence at Maidstone
East Hampton, New York, 1997–1999

Associate Partner: Randy M. Correll. Senior Assistant: Sarah Newbery. Assistants: Sharn Forster, Rebecca Laubach.

Apartment Tower at Sixty-Fifth Street and Third Avenue
New York, New York, 1997–2000

Associate Partner: Barry Rice. Project Associate: Michael Jones. Senior Assistant: Dennis Giobbe. Interiors Assistant: Damion Phillips. Associate Architect: Ismael Leyva Architects.

RiverVue
Tuckahoe, New York, 1997–

Associate Partner: Grant Marani. Project Associate: John Berson. Senior Assistant: John Cays. Assistants: Carolyn Foug, Jonas Goldberg, Dana Gulling.

The Seville
New York, New York, 1997–

Associate Partner: Barry Rice. Project Associate: Michael Jones. Assistant: Hernan Chebar. Associate Architect: Schuman Lichtenstein Claman & Efron.

South Station
Boston, Massachusetts, 1997

Partner: Graham S. Wyatt. Associate Partner: Alexander P. Lamis. Associates: Gary Brewer, Michael Jones. Senior Assistant: Anselm Fusco.

Illustration Credits

400   Assistants: Kurt Glauber, Dennis Sagiev, Tom VanDeWeghe, Youngmin Woo.

Senior Community
Celebration, Florida, 1997–

Partner: Paul Whalen. Project Associate: Daniel Lobitz. Senior Assistant: Quincey Nixon. Assistants: Maijinn Chen, Johnny Cruz, Carmen Gonzalez, Alex de Looz, Charles Toothill. Interiors Assistant: Damion Phillips. Landscape Associate: Charlotte M. Frieze. Landscape Assistant: Gerrit Goss. Associate Architect: Mann, Gin, Ebel & Frazier, Ltd.

Animation and Emerging Technologies Building, Sheridan College
Oakville-Trafalgar, Ontario, Canada, 1997

Associate Partner: Barry Rice. Assistants: Tamie Noponen, Michael Wilbur.

Arts Center, Denison University
Granville, Ohio, 1998–

Project Associate: Adam Anuszkiewicz. Senior Assistant: Michael Wilbur.

Residence
Palo Alto, California, 1998–

Associate Partner: Grant Marani. Senior Assistant: Carolyn Foug.

House for *This Old House* Magazine
Wilton, Connecticut, 1998–1999

Project Associate: Gary Brewer. Assistants: Deborah Cohen, Shannon Gallagher, Haven Knight.

Jenny Allen, "Dream House," *This Old House*, July–August 1998, 74–81.

Reforma 350
Mexico City, Mexico, 1998–1999

Partner: Graham S. Wyatt. Senior Assistant: Meghan McDermott. Assistants: Ryan Hullinger, John Mueller, Renan Pierre.

Public Library of Nashville and Davidson County
Nashville, Tennessee, 1998–2001

Associate Partner: Alexander P. Lamis. Senior Assistants: Jeffery Povero, Paul Zembsch. Assistants: Mark Gage, Melissa Del Vecchio, Ryan Hullinger, Michael Flaherty. Interiors Assistant: Claire Ratliff. Landscape Assistant: Laura Hynes.

Christine Kreyling, "Booking Space: Who'll Design the New Library?," *Nashville Scene*, April 9, 1998, 16–21, 23–24.

Rob Moritz, "Library Designs Down to 3," *Tennessean*, June 23, 1998, 1, 2.

Elizabeth S. Betts, "Some Architects Rate Top Design as Timeless, Others as Timeworn," *Tennessean*, June 25, 1998, 2.

Bonna M. de la Cruz, "Library Steals Page from Classics," *Tennessean*, June 25, 1998, 1.

Christing Kreyling, "In Limited Edition: The Library Designs Were Intriguing—But Who Saw Them?," *Nashville Scene*, June 25, 1998, 18–21.

Photography
Peter Aaron/Esto: 12–15, 16 (2), 17–21, 32–33, 40–45, 46–49, 50–55, 56–57, 65–69, 84–85, 88, 98–105, 116–23, 141–45, 154 (1), 155, 158–59, 162–63 (4), 166 (10), 169, 170–73, 194–201, 217–21, 235–39, 242–43, 272–77, 281–85; © The Celebration Company: 93–97; © The Walt Disney Company, used by permission: 107–15, 178–81, 182 (10, 12), 184–89, 264–87

© Baldinger Lighting Company, used by permission: 203

Jeff Botz: 156–57

Steven Brooke: 78–83, 124–29; courtesy of *Architectural Digest*, © 1995, The Condé Nast Publications, Inc., all rights reserved: 58–63, 148 (3), 149; courtesy of *Architectural Digest*, © 1998, The Condé Nast Publications, Inc., all rights reserved: 255–59

© The Celebration Company: 90–91

Jim Chapman: 207

© HBF, used by permission: 202

Kawasumi Architectural Photograph Office: 70–77

Robert Miller, © The Walt Disney Company, used by permission: 182 (11), 183

Jock Pottle/Esto: 231–33, 261–63, 332–33

Robert Reck: 22–29, 34–39

© Sasaki, used by permission: 205

Y. Takase/Yukio Futagawa and Associated Photographers: 154 (2)

Addison Thompson: 86–87, 89

Renderings
James Akers: 353

Joel Barkley: 208–9, 303, 307

Ernest Burden, III: 138–39, 212–13, 293, 326–27, 335, 365, 370–71

Joong-Seek Lee: 251

John Libertino: 350–51

John Mason: 343, 346, 379

Michael McCann: 354–55 (1–3), 372–73, 381

Emery Roth, Architect: 358 (1)

Chris Scarpati: 161, 165

Thomas Schaller: 318–19, 357, 366–67, 384–89

Timothy Slattery: 151, 177, 329

Clark Smith: 191, 316–17, 360–61, 363, 368, 377; © The Walt Disney Company, used by permission: 304–5

Dick Sneary, © The Walt Disney Company, used by permission: 297 (4)

Andrew Zega: 131, 136–37, 174–75, 210

Life is a registered trademark of Time Inc.